Sheffield Hallam University
Learning and IT Services
Collegiate Learning Centre
Collegiate Crescent Campus
Sheffield S10 2BP

101 929 534 1

Di

Sheffield Hallam University
Learning and Information Services
Withdrawn From Stock

CRITICAL AMERICA

General Editors: Richard Delgado and Jean Stefancic

White by Law: The Legal Construction of Race
Ian F. Haney López

Cultivating Intelligence: Power, Law, and the Politics of Teaching
Louise Harmon and Deborah W. Post

Privilege Revealed: How Invisible Preference Undermines America
Stephanie M. Wildmand with Margalynne Armstrong, Adrienne D. Davis, and Trina Grillo

Does the Law Morally Bind the Poor? or What Good's the Constitution When You Can't Afford a Loaf of Bread?
R. George Wright

Hybrid: Bisexuals, Multiracials, and Other Misfits under American Law
Ruth Colker

Critical Race Feminism: A Reader
Edited by Adrien Katherine Wing

Immigrants Out! The New Nativism and the Anti-Immigrant Impulse in the United States
Edited by Juan F. Perea

Taxing America
Edited by Karen B. Brown and Mary Louise Fellows

Notes of a Racial Caste Baby: Color Blindness and the End of Affirmative Action
Bryan K. Fair

Please Don't Wish Me a Merry Christmas: A Critical History of the Separation of Church and State
Stephen M. Feldman

To Be an American: Cultural Pluralism and the Rhetoric of Assimilation
Bill Ong Hing

Negrophobia and Reasonable Racism: The Hidden Costs of Being Black in America
Jody David Armour

Black and Brown in America: The Case for Cooperation
Bill Piatt

Black Rage Confronts the Law
Paul Harris

Selling Words: Free Speech in a Commercial Culture
R. George Wright

The Color of Crime: Racial Hoaxes, White Fear, Black Protectionism, Police Harassment, and Other Macroaggressions
Katheryn K. Russell

The Smart Culture: Society, Intelligence, and Law
Robert L. Hayman, Jr.

Was Blind, But Now I See: White Race Consciousness and the Law
Barbara J. Flagg

The Gender Line: Men, Women, and the Law
Nancy Levit

Heretics in the Temple: Americans Who Reject the Nation's Legal Faith
David Ray Papke

The Empire Strikes Back: Outsiders and the Struggle over Legal Education
Arthur Austin

Interracial Justice: Conflict and Reconciliation in Post–Civil Rights America
Eric K. Yamamoto

Black Men on Race, Gender, and Sexuality: A Critical Reader
Edited by Devon Carbado

When Sorry Isn't Enough: The Controversy over Apologies and Reparations for Human Injustice
Edited by Roy L. Brooks

Disoriented: Asian Americans, Law, and the Nation State
Robert S. Chang

Rape and the Culture of the Courtroom
Andrew E. Taslitz

The Passions of Law
Edited by Susan A. Bandes

Global Critical Race Feminism: An International Reader
Edited by Adrien Katherine Wing

Law and Religion: Critical Essays
Edited by Stephen M. Feldman

Changing Race: Latinos, the Census, and the History of Ethnicity
Clara E. Rodríguez

From the Ground Up: Environmental Racism and the Rise of the Environmental Justice Movement
Luke Cole and Sheila Foster

Nothing but the Truth: Why Trial Lawyers Don't, Can't, and Shouldn't Have to Tell the Whole Truth
Steven Lubet

Critical Race Theory: An Introduction
Richard Delgado and Jean Stefancic

Playing It Safe: How the Supreme Court Sidesteps Hard Cases
Lisa A. Kloppenberg

Why Lawsuits Are Good for America: Disciplined Democracy, Big Business, and the Common Law
Carl T. Bogus

How the Left Can Win Arguments and Influence People: A Tactical Manual for Pragmatic Progressives
John K. Wilson

Aftermath: The Clinton Impeachment and the Presidency in the Age of Political Spectacle
Edited by Leonard V. Kaplan and Beverly I. Moran

Getting over Equality: A Critical Diagnosis of Religious Freedom in America
Steven D. Smith

Critical Race Narratives: A Study of Race, Rhetoric, and Injury
Carl Gutiérrez-Jones

Social Scientists for Social Justice: Making the Case against Segregation
John P. Jackson, Jr.

Victims in the War on Crime: The Use and Abuse of Victims' Rights
Markus Dirk Dubber

Original Sin: Clarence Thomas and the Failure of the Constitutional Conservatives
Samuel A. Marcosson

Policing Hatred: Law Enforcement, Civil Rights, and Hate Crime
Jeannine Bell

Destructive Messages: How Hate Speech Paves the Way for Harmful Social Movements
Alexander Tsesis

Moral Imperialism: A Critical Anthology
Edited by Berta Esperanza Hernández-Truyol

In the Silicon Valley of Dreams: Environmental Injustice, Immigrant Workers, and the High-Tech Global Economy
David N. Pellow and
Lisa Sun-Hee Park

Mixed Race America and the Law: A Reader
Kevin R. Johnson

Critical Race Feminism: A Reader, Second Edition
Edited by Adrien Katherine Wing

Murder and the Reasonable Man: Passion and Fear in the Criminal Courtroom
Cynthia K. Lee

Success without Victory: Lost Legal Battles and the Long Road to Justice in America
Jules Lobel

Greasers and Gringos: Latinos, Law, and the American Imagination
Steven W. Bender

Saving Our Children from the First Amendment
Kevin W. Saunders

Elusive Citizenship: Immigration, Asian Americans, and the Paradox of Civil Rights
John S. W. Park

Truth, Autonomy, and Speech: Feminist Theory and the First Amendment
Susan H. Williams

Legal Education and the Reproduction of Hierarchy: A Polemic against the System, A Critical Edition
Duncan Kennedy,
with commentaries by Paul Carrington,
Peter Gabel, Angela Harris and
Donna Maeda, and Janet Halley

America's Colony: The Political and Cultural Conflict between the United States and Puerto Rico
Pedro A. Malavet

Alienated: Immigrant Rights, the Constitution, and Equality in America
Victor C. Romero

The Disability Pendulum: The First Decade of the Americans with Disabilities Act
Ruth Colker

Lawyers' Ethics and the Pursuit of Social Justice: A Critical Reader
Edited by Susan D. Carle

Rethinking Commodification: Cases and Readings in Law and Culture
Edited by Martha M. Ertman
and Joan C. Williams

The Derrick Bell Reader
Edited by Richard Delgado
and Jean Stefancic

Science for Segregation: Race, Law, and the Case against Brown v. Board of Education
John P. Jackson Jr.

Discrimination by Default: How Racism Becomes Routine
Lu-in Wang

Discrimination by Default

How Racism Becomes Routine

Lu-in Wang

NEW YORK UNIVERSITY PRESS
New York and London

New York University Press
New York and London
www.nyupress.org

© 2006 by New York University
All rights reserved

First published in paperback in 2008

Library of Congress Cataloging-in-Publication Data
Wang, Lu-in.
Discrimination by default : how racism becomes routine / Lu-in Wang.
p. cm. — (Critical America)
Includes bibliographical references and index.
ISBN–13: 978–0–8147–9447–0 (pbk. : alk. paper)
ISBN–10: 0–8147–9447–5 (pbk. : alk. paper)
ISBN–13: 978–0–8147–9379–4 (cloth : alk. paper)
ISBN–10: 0–8147–9379–7 (cloth : alk. paper)
1. Race discrimination—Law and legislation—United States.
2. Equality before the law—United States. I. Title. II. Series.
KF4755.W36 2005
342.7308'73—dc22 2005020721

New York University Press books are printed on acid-free paper, and their binding materials are chosen for strength and durability.

Manufactured in the United States of America

c 10 9 8 7 6 5 4 3 2 1
p 10 9 8 7 6 5 4 3 2 1

For Dave

Contents

Acknowledgments

This slim volume was a long time in the writing and benefited from the support and critiques of a number of people. Richard Delgado and Jean Stefancic have my heartfelt gratitude and admiration—first, for suggesting that I submit a book proposal for their wonderful series with NYU Press, and second, for their unflagging enthusiasm, their generous, thoughtful, and wise advice, and their persistent faith in me, which they seemed to maintain even when that faith was sorely tested. My editor, Jennifer Hammer, was unfailingly patient and supportive and helped this project along tremendously.

Many of my colleagues and friends read parts of earlier drafts and provided valuable comments and ideas; many thanks to Deborah Brake, Martha Chamallas (my first and best mentor), David Harris, Anne Lawton, Martha Mannix, Tom Ross, Stella Smetanka, George Taylor, and Welsh White. I also thank Mike Madison and Matt Shames for translating techie concepts into human ones, and Maraleen Shields, Jess Sommer, and Arthur Wolfson for their excellent research assistance. At the University of Pittsburgh School of Law, librarians Michele Kristakis and Susan Broms, along with their staff of research fellows, were invaluable and resourceful allies.

I benefited greatly from comments I received on this work at symposia or faculty workshops at DePaul University College of Law, Roger Williams University School of Law, Washington and Lee University School of Law, and the Law and Society Association annual meeting. This work also received generous support from the Dean's Scholarship fund at the University of Pittsburgh School of Law.

An earlier version of large portions of chapters 2, 3, 5, and 6 originally appeared as an article, Lu-in Wang, "Race as Proxy: Situational Racism and Self-Fulfilling Stereotypes," 53 *DePaul L. Rev.* 1013 (2004). I am grateful to the editors and staff of the *DePaul Law Review* for their work on that article and for the superb and thought-provoking symposium they organized on the topic of Race as Proxy.

Finally, I thank my parents, Li-jen and Jin Tsai Wang, and my children, An-Li and Maia Herring, for their encouragement and love. The largest measure of thanks goes to my spouse and colleague, Dave Herring, for supporting me in a variety of ways, including reading every word of the manuscript and understanding that, sometimes, being strategically unsympathetic was the most helpful thing he could do.

1

Discrimination by Default, Discrimination as Default

Alex arrived at the restaurant a bit early to meet his friends Tony and Jacqueline, but he hoped to get a table, relax, and unwind with a drink while he waited. The hostess who greeted him told him that would not be possible, as the restaurant's policy was that all members of a party had to be present before the party could be seated. She offered to take his name and said she could seat his party once everyone had arrived. Although he was anxious to be seated and the restaurant was only half full, Alex reluctantly agreed to wait on the hard bench in the entryway until his friends arrived.

As he sat waiting, several other diners entered and were seated. A White couple walked in and told the hostess they would have a party of four, but their two friends would be arriving later. Alex watched in disbelief as the hostess smiled and immediately showed the couple to a table. By the time the hostess returned to her station, Alex was furious. He strode over to her and announced in a loud voice that she could remove his name from the waiting list; he wasn't about to lower himself by patronizing a restaurant that treated him like a second-class citizen because he was Black.

The hostess reacted with surprise and anger. She protested that she was not a racist and had not treated him any differently because of his race; she had seated the couple right away because they were "regulars" and she did not want to make them wait in the cold entry hall for their friends. Alex, embarrassed and confused, left the restaurant.

Mary and Todd joined their law firm at the same time, as associates fresh out of law school, and were both assigned (along with a couple of more experienced associates) to work with Dan, a demanding but reputedly brilliant senior partner, on a high-profile case that was to go to trial in a few months. Dan's style was highly collaborative: he would hold frequent team meetings for all the lawyers on a case, at which they would brainstorm on strategies and arguments. Based on their performance at these meetings, Dan would choose one or two junior associates to take on significant roles at the trial itself—arguing a motion or two, examining or even cross-examining a couple of witnesses—quite a generous approach compared to some of his more rigid, hierarchical partners who tended to keep all the in-court work for themselves.

Mary was thrilled to be chosen for Dan's team and put in long hours doing legal research and combing through documents. Her initial enthusiasm began to wane after a few team meetings, however. Mary noticed that whenever she suggested an idea, the other lawyers seemed to ignore it and Dan would frequently dismiss it out of hand. Invariably, however, Todd would make the very same suggestion later in the meeting, to quite a different reception: the other lawyers would nod and smile, and, more often than not, Dan would accept the idea and praise Todd for suggesting it.

Mary soon grew discouraged and, after a while, gave up on offering suggestions in favor of simply doing the tasks that Dan assigned her at the end of each meeting. She was not surprised when the trial neared and Dan selected Todd over her to present one of the more important motions to the court. She overheard Dan telling Todd that he was "going to be a star some day." In contrast, when Mary met with Dan to discuss one of her research assignments, he told her that her work so far had been solid and thorough, but that she "really needed to start showing some initiative" by "thinking out of the box" and coming up with some creative ideas. Mary left Dan's office feeling frustrated and bewildered.

Professor Smith had a strict attendance policy for her undergraduate psychology class: students who missed more than five classes would be dropped from the course. The professor retained her discretion to excuse absences, but in her syllabus she warned students not to count on her mercy. James, a White sophomore, had already missed five classes when his unreliable Ford Escort broke down again, causing him to miss a sixth class. That same day, Li, also a sophomore, incurred her sixth absence as well. Li was a Chinese immigrant and the only member of her extended family who spoke fluent English. That day it had fallen to her, as it always did, to accompany her grandmother to a doctor's appointment so she could translate. Although she tried very hard to make it back to school in time for class, the appointment ran over and Li got to campus just after class had ended.

When James called the professor to explain why he had missed class and to plead for mercy, she laughed sympathetically. She had suffered plenty of car trouble when she was a student, she told him, so she'd let him go this time—but he had better start taking the bus from now on. As the professor hung up the phone, Li knocked on her office door. Li apologized for missing class that day, promised it wouldn't happen again, and asked the professor to please give her another chance. Professor Smith shook her head solemnly and said, in a kind but sad voice, "Li, you really need to start planning better. I'm afraid I can't excuse this absence because this has happened too many times already. I'm very sorry." Li was unhappy with this response, but had expected it. She'd have to register for an extra class the next semester to make up for the credits she would lose after being dropped from this one.

Are these three cases of discrimination? Did the hostess intend to treat Alex differently from the White couple because of his race, the senior partner intend to treat Mary differently from Todd because of her gender, or the professor intend to treat Li differently from James because of her ethnicity? While the answer to the first question may very well be yes, the answers to the next three may be no. That is, it may be that in each of the three cases the decision maker treated the other person less favorably than he or she would have if that person were of a different race, gender, or ethnicity—but that in none of the three cases did the decision maker intend to do so. It may be, in other words, that each of them discriminated not by design, but by default.

What does it mean to discriminate by default? Discrimination by default can take multiple forms and operate through multiple mechanisms, much like other default processes with which we are familiar.

The word "default" itself encompasses a wide range of meanings; it can be used as a noun, a verb, an adjective, or an adverb; and it can be read as negative, neutral, or positive. More traditional sources, like my 1986 *Webster's Ninth New Collegiate Dictionary*, define the word in mostly negative terms, equating default with failure: failure to pay a debt, failure to appear at a required legal proceeding, failure to compete in or complete an athletic contest.[1] In this sense of the word, when someone defaults bad things follow: a mortgage goes into foreclosure, a defendant must pay a legal judgment, a tennis player loses the match. Even in its negative sense, however, a default does not connote ill will or bad purpose, but rather a passive kind of failing: to default is to be remiss, negligent, forgetful, or simply incapable of meeting a requirement or challenge.

A default can be entirely neutral, as well. In this sense, a default is simply an automatic selection: what will be chosen in the absence of some action to prevent it. Mechanical devices like thermostats and appliances often have default settings to which they turn automatically if the user does not change them manually. Likewise, some defaults are viewed as unobjectionable in the legal world: default rules or contract terms, for example, are legal fallback settings that apply in the absence of a choice otherwise.

Defaults can carry positive connotations as well. Default rules and contract terms may be designated as such because long use of those standards has persuaded legal decision makers that they are the most fair or efficient among several alternatives. Default settings on appliances may be the ones that address the needs of most users or correspond with the optimal or safest modes of operation.

Those of us who use computers will recognize the full range of these meanings in the adoption of default settings on our computers. Our computers, and the software programs we use with them, have numerous default settings—far more than all but the most technologically savvy among us realize. Many of us accept almost all these settings, some because we have no preference otherwise, and some because we don't realize we have a choice. In this situation, our failure to take action literally may be the result of our neglect or failure, but acceptance of the default seems for the most part to be neutral or unobjectionable. In some cases, the choice made by default may even seem desirable, to the extent that the default setting is viewed as the expected, the best, or the most popular setting.

In many ways, it seems right that to choose a setting by default (or, more precisely, to *not choose* a different setting) should be viewed as positive. It is often simply more efficient and pleasant to adopt the standard setting than to spend undue amounts of time and thought trying to identify the best among several alternatives. Having too many choices can paralyze people, make it harder for them to decide among alternatives, raise their expectations unrealistically high, and leave them less satisfied with the decisions they do make.[2] Especially for the technologically challenged computer user, it may be not just easier but also safer to go with the default settings—and indeed, some software installation programs recommend that less experienced or sophisticated users leave well enough alone and opt for the vendor's preselected features. I, for one, am happy to comply. Further, and perhaps most obviously, the greater the number of people who use the default settings, the more compatible and consistent their work products will be, and the more efficiently and seamlessly the various parts of a team effort can be integrated into a whole.

But there are downsides to choices made by default, as well. First, the way in which defaults are established may not be ideal. Software engineers or web designers might strive to select defaults that are logical, promote ease of use, or reflect their sense of what most users would prefer. In some cases, however, the selection may be arbitrary or idiosyncratic, based more on the designer's personal, possibly quirky preferences than on her sense of what would work best for or appeal to most users. Even if the designer hopes to make a selection that is optimal for users, she may base that judgment on no more than her intuitive sense, discussions with her colleagues, or the responses of a small test or focus group, rather than a more scientific or broad-ranging analysis. All these methods can be influenced by the preferences, backgrounds, and biases of those individuals, which may not match those of most, or even typical, users. In the legal world, similarly, default rules might be biased in favor of the interests or preferences of those who have developed them—usually those who already hold the most power in the legal system and society.[3]

The designation of a default might even be manipulative and harmful, as arguably is the case with web browsers that are delivered with a default setting to allow "cookies"—small text files that store information on a computer's hard drive—to be written and read without the user's awareness or consent. Private data-mining companies take advantage of this default setting to collect and analyze a vast array of personal information on Internet users, because they can use the cookies that are stored on a hard drive to track the user's movements on the Internet. Through this surveillance, such companies can create detailed profiles of hundreds of millions of Internet users—a dream for marketing companies and other businesses that want to enhance their sales by learning more about consumers, but a nightmare to privacy advocates and those whose interests they represent.[4]

Furthermore, decisions made by default can themselves simply reflect bad decision making—or no decision making at all. People sometimes don't realize that a particular default feature has been set and would not want it if they did. Because cookies can be placed invisibly and most people are unaware that their browsers have been set to allow this process, millions of Internet users unwittingly permit companies to collect personal, potentially sensitive information on them that they might prefer not to share.

The appeal of the default can be magnified or distorted by the user's desire to avoid dealing with information to which she really should be attending. First, because the user must expend effort to choose something other than the default setting, to make another choice entails costs that have to be overcome. The more complicated or less familiar the situation, the more people tend to fall back with relief on the default, as a way of dodging a difficult decision or task. Although software and website designers striving for ease of use are exhorted to heed the command, "Don't make me think!"[5] the choice that requires the least thought is not always the best, and complicated situations might be the least appropriate ones in which to make a decision by default. Default cookie settings again provide an illustration. While these settings are, as described above, likely not desirable for many users, most will not bother to change them, either because they do not realize they should or because it is too difficult or confusing to do so.[6]

A user who tries to change from the default setting might even be discouraged from doing so by a chain of complications that change can set off. One writer has recounted, for example, the roadblocks he encountered when he tried to increase the privacy setting of his new web browser from the default setting of Medium to the next one up, Medium High: when he attempted to log onto the Internet after changing the privacy setting, he received a message warning him that the setting he had chosen might interfere with the functioning of some features of the browser and "recommend[ing] that [his] privacy setting be configured to the default."[7]

Whether it is a good or bad choice, the default setting tends to become entrenched as the *standard* setting, thereby perpetuating and magnifying its influence.[8] That is, the default can attain dominance through the accumulation of users and the passage of time. A simple but recognizable example of the power of the default to set the standard is the rise of the Times New Roman font. This font style has become de rigueur for a wide range of documents, both real and virtual, but this was not always the case. For many years, the Courier font was standard, especially for legal and other official papers. Courier itself came into prominence because it was used in the "golf ball" typing head technology for IBM's electric typewriters. Over the years, however, as computers have overtaken typewriters as our primary means of producing documents, Times New Roman has supplanted Courier. The changing of the standard has been due in no small part to the fact that Times New Roman is the default font for widely used word processing programs such as Microsoft Word and Corel WordPerfect. The supremacy of Times New Roman was confirmed when, in February 2004, the State Department declared that Courier was "obsolete" and henceforth banned for use in most official documents. Instead, all official correspondence was from then on to be set in the "crisper, cleaner, more modern" Times New Roman.[9]

Discrimination by Default, Discrimination as Default

Modern-day discrimination resembles decision making by default to a remarkable degree and in all its senses: the neglect or failure that is implied in the traditional use of the word, as well as the automaticity, passivity, and potential suboptimality of "selecting" a computer setting by default. And, as often happens when most of us accept the default setting on a computer, discrimination *by* default creates a situation in which that discrimination *becomes* the default: the expected, the accepted, the standard. Once it becomes the standard, we take it for granted and fail to recognize the extent to which it influences how we operate in the world.

First, like a default in the traditional sense, we often discriminate through failure or neglect, reaching a bad result not through ill will or evil purpose, but because we are unaware of our failing or are incapable of doing differently. Social psychologists have shown, for example, that most people are afflicted with unconscious cognitive and motivational biases that lead us reflexively to categorize, perceive, interpret the behavior of, remember, and interact with people of different groups differently. These unconscious biases, in turn, can lead us to treat people differently based on race and other irrelevant characteristics without intending to or even being aware that we are doing so.

In his recent (2005) bestseller, *Blink*, Malcolm Gladwell recounts the devastating consequences that unconscious bias wreaked during the fateful "seven seconds in the Bronx" that resulted in the death of Amadou Diallo.[10] The story of Diallo's death is well known: late on the night of February 3, 1999, four plainclothes police officers cruising Wheeler Avenue in the Bronx spotted a young Black man standing in a doorway, acting in a way that, to them, appeared suspicious. Diallo stood on the stoop, peeking in and out, scanning the block. The officer who was driving backed up the car so that it stopped right in front of Diallo's building. Diallo stayed in place, another behavior the officers found odd because it seemed so brazen. Two officers got out of the car, and one held up his badge and asked, "Can we have a word?" Diallo said nothing, paused, and then ran into the vestibule. The two officers ran after him. Diallo grabbed the knob of the inner door with his left hand, at the same time turning his body sideways and "digging" into his pocket with his right hand. One officer yelled at him to "Show me your hands!" while the other shouted: "Get your hands out of your pockets! Don't make me fucking kill you!" Diallo continued to dig in his pocket, growing "more and more agitated." He then turned, looked at the officers, and pulled a black object from his pocket. One officer shouted, "Gun! He's got a gun!" and then chaos erupted. The story's ending is all too familiar. The two officers began shooting their semiautomatic weapons at Diallo as their colleagues ran toward the building firing their weapons. Within seconds, forty-one shots had been fired, nineteen had struck Diallo, and he lay dead—holding in his outstretched hand not a gun, but his wallet.[11]

The officers—themselves "raw[,] new to the Bronx and new to the Street Crime Unit and new to the unimaginable stresses of chasing what they think is an armed man down a darkened hallway"[12]—made a number of mistakes that night. The first was seeing Diallo's initial posture—standing in the doorway, getting some air—as suspicious. The second was seeing his reaction to their movements—staying in place, watching them as they backed up the car and stopped it in front of him—as brazen, when he was probably just curious. The final, fatal mistake was in reading Diallo's next steps—turning toward the door, digging into his pocket as they approached him—as dangerous.[13] Diallo was not dangerous, he was terrified. As an immigrant, he most likely reached for his wallet so he could show the officers his identification papers.

Gladwell points out that neither of the two popular explanations provides a satisfying account of the Diallo case. This was not "an open-and-shut case of racism," for no evidence suggests that the officers involved were "bad people, or racists, or out to get Diallo." Nor was it "just a horrible accident, an inevitable by-product of the fact that police officers sometimes have to make life-or-death decisions in conditions of uncertainty," as the jury in the officers' criminal case concluded. Instead, Gladwell proposes, the Diallo case "falls into a kind of gray area, the middle ground between deliberate and accidental," in which "[t]he officers made a series of critical misjudgments, beginning with the assumption that a man getting a breath of fresh air outside his own home was a potential criminal."[14]

The gray area that Gladwell describes is the space into which unconscious biases and reflexive judgments fall. Diallo's race played a crucial part in determining how the officers interpreted his actions, but not because the officers intentionally sought to target, shoot, and kill a Black man. They believed Diallo was suspicious, believed he was pulling a gun, believed their lives were in danger, all because his Black skin primed them to see those things when they looked at him.[15] The officers, in other words, indeed discriminated against Diallo, but they discriminated more by default than by design.

Even when the results are not so heartbreakingly apparent, unconscious bias can have substantial, material consequences because it permeates our behavior in a wide range of ordinary situations. Whether a defendant is found guilty or goes free, whether a driver is pulled over or allowed to travel unimpeded, whether a candidate gets a job or is rejected, and even how much a consumer pays for a good, all might depend on that person's race, ethnicity, gender, or other irrelevant characteristics, because all might be influenced by the kinds of unconscious bias that caused those officers to see a gun where Diallo held his wallet.

We may not notice the disparities that result from these biases because we may take the outcomes, and the practices that produce them, for granted. Our social environment supports discrimination by default because, in many ways, it has set discrimination *as* the default. Our individual biases dovetail with a set of social practices, patterns, and norms that produce and reproduce unintentional discrimination and have become so familiar that they define our sense of what is "normal," and, in turn, what is "real" and even "natural."[16] For example, when the people who are in power—politicians, judges, business and civic leaders—appoint others to prominent committees and positions, we expect them to select among individuals they already know, through their churches, clubs, board memberships, and other such circles, and they generally do. As a result, more affluent White men than women, racial minorities, or poor people tend to end up in powerful positions. This outcome does not surprise us and, at least until some recent episodes of consciousness-raising, has not tended to draw much attention. We expect and accept these outcomes—largely because we do not recognize them as discriminatory, but instead as simply the way things are: standard operating conditions.

Discrimination then becomes part of the very structure of our society, as the default we have come to accept first achieves dominance and then perpetuates that dominance through the self-reinforcing advantages of its status. Again, computer technology provides the analogy. Legal scholars borrowing from antitrust theory have shown that Whiteness, in particular, has become a durable monopoly through dynamics much like those that have contributed to the market power of the Microsoft Windows operating system. Despite arguably *not* being the best operating system available, Windows dominates because:

> (1) the more people there are who own Windows, the more attractive it is for others to own it; (2) the more Windows users there are, the more likely it is that more software applications will be offered by other firms that run on Windows; (3) the more firms there are that use Windows, the more useful it becomes to learn Windows skills; (4) the more people there are in the world using Windows, the more useful it is to operate a system with disks, protocols, and file formats that are compatible with Windows; and (5) the more Windows applications, Windows-trained personnel, and Windows-compatible systems there are in the world, the more inexorable the conclusion that one must own a computer system that runs on Windows, even if you think it is an impossibly buggy and sluggish system. Network economics makes Windows an indispensable product.[17]

As this elaboration of Windows's rise suggests, once a product becomes the de facto standard, that "small initial advantage can translate into enduring market dominance" if the market is characterized by "positive feedback loops" that reflect, reinforce, and lock in that dominance.[18] Likewise, when discrimination against nondominant groups becomes a default practice, the dominant group—Whites, to take the most analyzed example—becomes the de facto, accepted, and taken for granted standard.

Whiteness *has* become the default race in our society: "People are presumed to be White unless otherwise stated. Thus the 'standard' judge, teacher, student, or customer—the standard person—is imagined to be White."[19] Like Windows, Whites enjoy a market and social environment characterized by networks that increase the initial advantage of being the accepted standard. That initial advantage may have been won through "deliberately anticompetitive conduct"[20]—racism, in plainer terms—including this country's history of slavery, segregation, and other overt discrimination, but the positive feedback loops that the dominant group enjoys provide an environment in which maintaining its dominance no longer *depends* on deliberate manipulations. Instead, the group's dominance perpetuates itself "naturally," through seemingly neutral preferences for language, culture, stereotypes, and credentials that are associated with the standard and exclude those who are, or are perceived to be, incompatible.

Consider the case of White dominance in the legal profession. Whiteness became the de facto standard in the profession through the intentional exclusion of non-Whites: the profession kept non-Whites out of legal education, and hence out of the profession, through "formal Jim Crow segregation laws and informal exclusionary policies," by moving legal education to the university setting and "from a skills-oriented program to science- and theory-based instruction" accessible only to White elites, and by eliminating "night, part-time, and private programs that catered to people of color and immigrants."[21]

The profession has maintained and reinforced White dominance by locking in that culturally specific standard, creating significant barriers to entry for people of color. Today, the single most important qualification for admission to law school, and hence for entry into the profession, is the Law School Admission Test, or LSAT. The LSAT arguably is not the best predictor of which students will be the best or most competent lawyers. The test assesses verbal and reasoning skills and rewards "rote performance, guessing, gamesmanship, and the ability to sort artificial alternatives quickly under timed conditions,"[22] but it does not measure a number of other abilities and qualities that a good lawyer should possess, such as "empathy, communication skills, common sense, reasoning by analogy, synthetic reasoning, . . . the ability to make order out of situations that are ambiguous, complex, and uncertain," or understanding of human motivation and psychology.[23] Nor do LSAT scores correlate with success as a lawyer: while they *might* (at least in combination with a student's undergraduate grade point average) be a good predictor of law school *grades*,[24] they *do not* appear to bear a significant relationship to *achievement* after law school graduation, whether measured by income, career satisfaction, or service to the profession and community.[25] In fact, LSAT scores correlate negatively with important qualities and behaviors to which lawyers are taught to aspire: "community activism, social empathy, a desire to help others in trouble, and wanting to make a contribution to knowledge."[26]

On the other hand, the test clearly does favor Whites and students from higher social classes and economic brackets, who tend as a group to score disproportionately higher on the LSAT than non-Whites and students of lower socioeconomic status.[27] The test is racially and culturally biased in part because LSAT scores reflect and lock in the relative advantages enjoyed by affluent Whites and the disadvantages suffered by poor non-Whites, such as inequalities in school funding, access to test preparation courses, and test-taking "savviness."[28] But the test itself is also at fault because it asks many questions that assume knowledge of topics that are familiar to middle- or upper-class Whites but not to poor or minority students.[29] As we will see, even the test-taking situation itself can introduce racial or cultural bias if it induces "stereotype threat"—a phenomenon that causes members of groups that are subject to negative stereotypes about their intellectual ability to perform more poorly on standardized tests when they are reminded of those stereotypes.[30]

Not surprisingly, when law school admissions committees base admissions decisions on LSAT scores, they exclude non-White applicants disproportionately, and law school classes continue to be disproportionately White.[31] The de facto White standard becomes further entrenched through the significant network benefits to which it connects. Because national rankings of law schools rely heavily on LSAT scores, admitting students with higher scores is a way for a law school to "signal the 'quality' of its program to a wide range of legal professionals—prospective employers and their clients, alumni, the legal community of practitioners at large, and other law schools."[32] Using the standard also makes it easier for law schools to signal "quality" to prospective students and to reach consensus among internal decision makers on admissions decisions. All these benefits have a mutually reinforcing effect: higher rankings attract higher "quality" students, greater employment opportunities and salaries for those students, and increased alumni giving to the school—all of which feed back on one another and "reinforce the success of the law school that chooses to admit on-standard applicants."[33]

At the same time, moreover, the de facto standard creates barriers to entry for those who do not conform to it, both by giving White students who do an advantage over students of color and by creating high "switching costs" for law schools that might consider changing to a different admissions standard. Among those switching costs are the competitive disadvantages that would accompany the change, such as a slide in the national rankings and in the regard of the relevant professional community.[34] As a result—and as I know firsthand as a member of a law school faculty that has wrestled with this question—even those decision makers who fully appreciate the effect of the default standard on people of color and decry its impact on our efforts to diversify our student bodies and improve the overall quality of the legal profession are hard-pressed to change to a different standard.

Once the dominant standard has been set, the discrimination and inequality it engenders can persist without any explicit or conscious effort to maintain it. However, "specific intent and determination [are] required to dislodge it."[35]

Situational Racism, Self-Fulfilling Stereotypes, and Failures of Imagination

As part of the struggle to dislodge the discriminatory standard, this book will illuminate three specific ways in which discrimination occurs by default and becomes the default. The following chapters highlight the capacity of our expectations to both promote and obscure discrimination, thereby reinforcing the expectation and acceptance of disparate treatment and outcomes. Collectively, these chapters argue that individual adjudication under the intentional model of discrimination—in which a defendant consciously intended to discriminate against another person based on race or other prohibited reason—is inadequate to redress the largest share of modern discrimination. Individual adjudication is inadequate because the situations in which discrimination is easy to see are not the ones in which it is most likely to be found, and because the discriminatory default has become standard, making it hard for us to imagine the alternative. Once we recognize these default dynamics, however, we can begin to develop ways to reduce their influence on legal determinations and fashion social, institutional, and structural approaches to disrupt them.

Social psychological research teaches three important lessons. First, discrimination is often more situation- and less character-driven than we tend to appreciate. More specifically, some situations can promote discrimination even while (and perhaps by) allowing that discrimination to escape notice, leading both the actor and observers to miss seeing it in precisely those situations in which it is most likely to occur. Second, group-based biases can channel our behavior to create the kinds of situations that promote and obscure discrimination. Third, biases in our reactions to events can lead us both to overlook discriminatory outcomes and to develop biased explanations for why bad things happen to different people. These explanations can, in turn, reinforce group-based biases by leading us to interpret discriminatory outcomes as appropriate or justified.

These processes and biases are subtle and operate largely by default. They are all variations on common, exceedingly normal, human failings. As we shall see, the same susceptibility to situational cues that causes us to overeat can lead us to treat a person of color more harshly than a White person; the same self-fulfilling process that causes us to "choke" when we feel vulnerable to failure can lead us to interact with a woman in a way that elicits gender-stereotyped responses from her; and the same preference for the familiar that causes us to sympathize more with a down-on-his-luck neighbor than with starving Biafrans can lead us to view discriminatory outcomes as just and proper. The hostess we saw at the beginning of the chapter who refused to seat Alex, the senior partner who failed to appreciate Mary's contributions, and the professor who took a hard line with Li each may have succumbed to one or more of these ways of discriminating by default.

Situational racism. Social psychological research shows that everyday situations can promote our defaulting to discrimination. In particular, people are more likely to discriminate in situations that are "normatively ambiguous": in which, for example, clearly negative behavior against a person of color can be justified or rationalized on some basis other than race. As a result, discrimination is *most likely to occur* in situations where it is *least likely to be detected.*

Furthermore, the individual who discriminates in such a situation may well do so without intention or awareness, because the situation can conceal the influence of racial bias from the perpetrator as well as the observer. As a result, the actor and observer—and even the victim of discrimination—may not realize what has happened and may view the actor's conduct not as racially biased but as entirely legitimate, and even desirable.

Self-fulfilling stereotypes. Social psychology also shows that situations are not purely "given." We are not passive inhabitants of our environment, but can actively, although often unwittingly, produce the very situations that seem to justify, and thereby mask, racially biased conduct. People can define situations in normatively ambiguous terms when we act on racial and other group-based stereotypes. Stereotypes can channel and constrain our behavior—how we approach and respond to one another—in a way that produces objective "evidence" to confirm the stereotype. As we shall see, moreover, the real power of racial stereotypes lies not so much in their ability to channel situations in this way, but in their ability to do so while concealing the role that they played.

Failures of imagination. Once the default is set, it becomes the standard, and events that are consistent with the standard seem right and appropriate. The third line of research, on counterfactual thinking and norm theory, shows that our reactions to and assessments of discrimination—which may include the failure to perceive discrimination—hinge on the way in which we reconstruct an event after it occurs. Our preference for what is normal predisposes us to sympathize more with those who typically suffer less and inures us to the pain of those whose suffering we expect. Accordingly, we are prone to overlook or underreact to discriminatory outcomes. In addition to accounting for our biased affective reactions to negative events, norm theory reveals our tendency to develop biased explanations for why bad things happen to people, which may result in undue tolerance of discriminatory practices. We also tend to blame victims of discrimination for the negative treatment they receive, especially if the victim acted in a way that challenges established practices or accepted stereotypes. Thus, our subsequent assessments of discriminatory outcomes may reinforce the perception that discriminatory outcomes are appropriate and justified.

We need to understand and disrupt these default mechanisms, because—like the network effects that lock in a monopoly gained through deliberate anticompetitive conduct—they work together with and support more explicit and intentional forms of discrimination. In combination, all these forces promote and obscure discriminatory outcomes by reinforcing the expectation of discrimination and maintenance of the status quo.

Consistent with my thesis, this book uses a broad definition of discrimination. It discusses a wide range of conduct and practices that are not typically treated together and that might or might not meet traditional legal standards for, or fit within popular, lay conceptions of, discrimination. These various forms of discrimination reflect the various meanings of "default" and range from obvious or prototypical examples of discrimination (such as hate crimes or sexual harassment), through the recognizable but arguably not illegitimate (such as racial profiling in law enforcement), to practices that we more controversially refer to as discrimination (such as the use of race or ethnicity as a diagnostic factor in medicine). Together, these varieties of discrimination support a social, cultural, and legal environment in which discrimination can easily occur by default, because discrimination often *is* the default.

Discrimination without Fault?

Legal prohibitions, our most obvious way of holding individuals and institutions accountable for discrimination, are not equipped to deal with these processes, because the law is not well suited to identify or correct problems that are produced by default. We do not generally impose liability for unintended, passive wrongs, or for wrongs that the defendant was not on notice he might be committing—even a default judgment cannot be entered unless the defendant had proper notice of the claim against him. Furthermore, the law generally does not find fault with, and often protects and approves of, someone who follows standard practices.

These general tendencies are especially pronounced in the legal standards governing claims of discrimination. Despite the wealth of antidiscrimination laws that would seem to prohibit racial and other group-based discrimination in a wide range of settings, much discriminatory decision making escapes legal sanction. Legal redress fails in part because of what one legal scholar has called a "fundamental 'lack of fit' between the jurisprudential construction of discrimination and the actual phenomenon it purports to represent."[36]

Scholars have been particularly critical of the prevailing model of intentional discrimination.[37] This model applies to almost all claims of racial or other group-based discrimination and requires the plaintiff to prove that the defendant consciously intended to discriminate against him or her "because of" race or some other prohibited reason. For example, the U.S. Supreme Court's equal protection doctrine requires the plaintiff to establish that the defendant had a "discriminatory purpose."[38] The Court has elaborated that this requirement is not satisfied by showing that the action complained of was taken "in spite of" its discriminatory effect; the plaintiff must prove that it was taken "*because of*" that effect. This requirement imposes a substantial burden on plaintiffs, for it is often exceedingly difficult to establish a defendant's purpose or motive.[39] Making the burden even heavier is the way in which courts have conceived of discriminatory "purpose": not only must the actor intend to treat the plaintiff differently because of his or her social group status, but that intent to discriminate must also incorporate animus or bad faith.[40] The dominant view is that "real" discrimination is perpetrated only by individuals who are motivated by hostility and seek to do harm to disfavored groups. That is, not only must the actor intentionally engage in conduct that is racially discriminatory, but he or she also must "be" a racist. This view divides the world into two types of decision makers: those who are motivated by racial animus and do discriminate, and those who are not motivated by animus and by definition do not discriminate.[41]

A sampling of legal discourse in different settings reveals this dichotomous thinking at work. With respect to racial profiling in law enforcement, the idea that police officers conducting stops, searches, and seizures can be neatly categorized as either racist transgressors or nonracist innocents underlies Supreme Court decisions that foreclose the Fourth Amendment, with its focus on whether the officer had probable cause or reasonable suspicion of criminal activity, as a source of legal remedy for racial profiling. The Court instead relegates claims of racial discrimination to the equal protection clause and its discriminatory purpose doctrine.[42] The Court's treatment of race in its famous cases of *Terry v. Ohio*[43] and *Whren v. United States*,[44] "divides the world of police officers into 'good cops' ([those] who can be trusted) and 'rogue cops' (the ones who might be expected to abuse whatever powers have been delegated to them),"[45] the latter being those who, for example, engage in the "'wholesale harassment' of minority groups."[46] Further, by erecting a doctrinal barrier between claims of racial discrimination and claims that a police officer lacked probable cause or reasonable suspicion for making a stop—thereby "removing race from Fourth Amendment analysis"—the Court's decisions have created a world in which we can distinguish not only between "good cops" and "rogue cops," but also between situations "in which there clearly is and those in which there clearly is not 'probable cause.'"[47] The Court has created "a reality in which it is possible to separate a police officer's racial bias from his or her observations and account of alleged criminality," thereby making it possible to see the officer's actions "as resting upon neutral facts untainted by racial bias."[48]

Similarly, disparate treatment doctrine in employment discrimination law under Title VII incorporates a "rhetoric of invidiousness" that is constructed on a set of assumptions about and interpretations of the actor's decision-making process that understand that process in stark, oversimplified terms.[49] As in equal protection doctrine, the law under Title VII requires that the plaintiff prove that she received differential treatment and that it resulted from purposeful or intentional discrimination. Further, and, "[p]articularly in the context of race and national origin, discrimination is represented as resulting from the decisionmaker's discriminatory *animus* towards members of the plaintiff's racial or ethnic group"—specifically, the desire to exclude members of certain groups from the workforce.[50] Thus, in order to discriminate unlawfully, the decision maker must be motivated by ill intentions: "there is no discrimination without an invidiously motivated actor. Every successful disparate treatment story needs a villain."[51] The assumption that the actor who discriminates was "invidiously motivated" leads to the converse assumption that employers who do not harbor such evil intent "will act objectively and judge rationally."[52] (This view leads to the further assumption that a decision maker who denies discriminating but has made a "suboptimal" decision must be lying about her reasons for making that decision.)[53] These two tracks of thinking are viewed as mutually exclusive and the employer as completely aware of her reasons for acting, so that her "true" reason for the employment decision can be categorized as *either* invidious and discriminatory *or* noninvidious and nondiscriminatory. The law requires that a choice be made between these two characterizations and recognizes no more complicated explanations.

This dichotomous, all-or-nothing model allows a large share of contemporary discrimination to escape legal sanction, or even notice. Decisions and conduct that are otherwise motivated will, of course, not be recognized as discriminatory. Perhaps not incidentally, individuals who *are* driven by bad intentions will find it easier to disguise that fact, for, as we shall see, the conventional view readily accepts defendants' proffered nondiscriminatory justifications for differential treatment, even when those justifications rest on thinly disguised stereotypes. Further, because of the default manner in which discrimination can so easily occur, many biased decisions may very well be unintended. Finally, the intent requirement does not capture disparate treatment that results from compliance with biased institutional norms and practices, thereby obscuring and protecting those patterns of discrimination that have become well established through repetition and tradition.

Traditional legal standards reflect and reinforce social definitions of discrimination—what might be called "folk theories" of discrimination[54]—as being conscious, deliberate, and based in a moral failing. The dominant legal model reflects and reinforces misconceptions about how discrimination usually occurs and, in doing so, stands in the way of meaningful social change. Furthermore, and as we shall see, many of the flaws in the legal model are the same flaws in thinking that contribute to discrimination itself. That is, the lens we use to detect discrimination distorts our assessments of racially disparate outcomes in much the same way that the lens through which we view the world distorts our perceptions of people and situations and leads us to discriminate. Together, these legal and social conceptions contribute to the institutionalization and entrenchment of discriminatory patterns by constructing discrimination in ways that make it hard to see, that dress it up as being acceptable or even desirable, or that resign us to living with a regrettable, but seemingly inevitable, state of affairs.

The direct consequence of the law's failure to appreciate the interacting influences of unconscious bias, institutional norms, and the default processes presented here is the inability of individuals to secure legal redress for their injuries when they have suffered losses as a result of discrimination that does not fit the traditional mold. A less obvious but no less serious consequence of the conventional model is that it stands in the way of meaningful social change and itself becomes a link in a feedback loop that perpetuates an artificial conception of bias. Traditional legal standards, in other words, are themselves part of the problem, to the extent that they direct attention to the search for invidiously motivated individual decision makers and away from the need and potential for institutional change—altering the "situation"—as a means of disrupting the noninvidious, "normal," but no less problematic routes by which we perpetrate and perpetuate discrimination.

Moreover, when we limit our focus and our condemnation to discrimination that can be characterized as deviant and invidiously motivated, we overlook discrimination that was influenced by the social environment or, even worse, justify that discrimination on "moral" grounds. As Charles Lawrence has explained: "[I]f there is no discrimination, there is no need for a remedy; if blacks are being treated fairly yet remain at the bottom of the socioeconomic ladder, only their own inferiority can explain their subordinate position."[55] In other words, the traditional, "perpetrator"-focused perspective itself perpetuates discrimination, for it institutionalizes the notion that much of the differential treatment of people of color is appropriate and even just.

We also may adopt the fatalistic view that much discrimination is "natural" and therefore not to be regulated, but instead to be expected and accepted. To some extent, this view incorporates an accurate description of how discrimination occurs. However, research shows that while all these processes can be characterized as "normal," they are hardly inevitable. They can be disrupted if we recognize them and have the desire and will to think and act differently. We can override the default.

2 Situational Racism

We think we can tell a lot about a person from her behavior, but in fact we make some of our biggest mistakes when we use people's actions as a basis for drawing conclusions about their character. Unfortunately for our attempts to address the age-old problem of discrimination, this mistake lies at the heart of both legal and social understandings of the way discrimination operates.

Traditional legal standards for discrimination reflect the influence of lay psychology on the way the law understands human behavior and assesses responsibility. The intentional model of discrimination is based on the common assumption that only a certain kind of person would discriminate. Because we believe that an individual's behavior is largely determined by his character, including his attitudes and beliefs, we do not just equate discrimination with an intent to discriminate but also assume that someone who discriminates has a "taste for discrimination": a preference that exists inside him, is stable, and directs his actions "consistently over time and across different situations."[1] As a result, we tend to believe that only someone who "is" prejudiced or racist would discriminate on an illegitimate basis, and to expect that someone who discriminated in one set of circumstances would do so in another—or, conversely, that someone who did *not* discriminate in one situation would not do so in another.[2]

This focus on character-based, internal explanations leads us to equate, and even to conflate, discrimination with bad character. Conversely, when we attribute disparate treatment to external or situational factors, we tend—as with other negative outcomes that we attribute to the situation—to view it as justified or understandable. Indeed, we may not even label it "discrimination" at all, but characterize it simply as a rational reaction to a particular set of objective facts. Thus, for example, a criminal who targets Asian immigrants for violence because of his hostility toward foreigners is considered to have committed a discriminatory "hate" crime, but one who targets Asian immigrant shopkeepers for robbery because he views them as easy targets or as unlikely to report the crime is viewed not as discriminating but as behaving as a rational robber naturally would.[3] A police officer who acts on a "hunch" in interpreting a Black motorist's behavior as suspicious—when the hunch is based on no more than a stereotype equating Blackness with criminality—is not engaging in discrimination but in "good police practice."[4]

Furthermore, the tendency to draw sharp distinctions between character- and situation-based explanations for others' behavior also introduces circularity into assessments of the acceptability of that behavior. People's expectations of how others typically behave in certain situations tend to skew their explanations for and judgments of others' behavior. Behavior that is unexpected or considered extreme tends to be attributed to the actor's character and is judged to be inappropriate or unjustified, while behavior that is expected or viewed as typical tends to be attributed to the situation and is judged as appropriate or justified.[5] The former bias may explain why people generally do condemn extreme acts of discrimination such as hate crimes, which they tend to attribute to the perpetrators' deviant character but not to situational influences. The converse tendency, in contrast, may explain why more mundane forms of discrimination are seen as acceptable. People may overlook the biased beliefs or attitudes that contribute to more ordinary kinds of discrimination such as racial profiling in law enforcement and instead see the practice as a response to the situation and therefore not discriminatory.

But the most basic error people make in assessing human behavior lies in drawing this distinction. We tend to see someone else's conduct as being mostly or even exclusively determined by *character* (the kind of person she is) while overlooking the *situation* in which the person is acting. This fundamental attribution error or correspondence bias is "[p]erhaps the most commonly documented bias in social perception" in Western cultures,[6] and causes us to draw erroneous inferences about people's characteristics and qualities from their behavior and to have unrealistic expectations for their behavior.[7] It leads us both to overemphasize the importance of character in determining another person's behavior and to expect people to behave consistently in different situations.

Internally focused, disposition-based inferences often are not warranted, especially when a person's behavior is consistent with incentives, constraints, pressures, or expectations introduced by the situation. For example, a teacher may be stern and businesslike in the classroom because he needs to cover assigned course material within the allotted time, rather than because of a generally no-nonsense personality. Nor do people always behave consistently across contexts, for different situations present different opportunities and limitations. The same teacher who is stern in the classroom may be kind and solicitous during office hours, when he is free of time pressure.

Moreover, if we tend generally to overlook situational influences on human behavior, we are especially prone to underappreciate the existence and effect of precisely the kinds of factors that most strongly influence discrimination. Social constraints such as roles, expectations, norms, and stereotypes can be powerful influences on a person's behavior and may be no less a feature of the situation than physical or temporal constraints, such as bad lighting or time pressures. But because they exist in the actor's brain and affect the actor's interpretation of the situation, these forces are often invisible to the observer.[8]

An individual's decision to treat people of different races differently does not necessarily reflect a basically racist personality, and an individual who discriminates on the basis of race in one setting may not do so in another. Whether a person discriminates may—and as we shall see, often does—depend on the situation.

"The Power of the Situation": Channel Factors, Helping and Harming

We often respond more readily to circumstances, and less to internal guides such as attitudes or beliefs, than might be expected. Moreover, seemingly trivial or subtle differences in the situation can produce substantial differences in behavior. How much we eat can be influenced more strongly by external factors such as how food is packaged, presented, or priced than by internal factors such as hunger or lack of will power.[9] Whether or not we get a flu shot as recommended each winter may depend more on the location and hours of the vaccination clinic than on our awareness of the benefits of receiving the inoculation, and our decision to donate to a particular charity may depend more on whether we receive a direct, personal request than on our agreement with the organization's cause.[10] Social psychologists call these small but mighty influences "channel factors" because of the critical role they play in directing behavior. First, a channel factor affects how an individual defines a situation—what kind of situation it is, what interests are at stake, and so forth; then, it "channels" his or her behavior by indicating the appropriate conduct for that situation, essentially opening or closing pathways for action.[11]

Even how we treat other people can be influenced more strongly by the situation than by our own dispositions. In a collection of now classic experimental studies, social psychologists discovered that what seem to be insignificant features of a situation can influence people to refrain from helping and even to actively mistreat others. Indeed, sometimes very mild constraints can lead people to engage in abusive conduct even when they do not wish to cause the other person harm and are distressed by the knowledge that they are doing so.

A variety of situational factors can inhibit or promote helping behavior. In a famous study inspired by the biblical parable of the Good Samaritan, seminary students were much more likely to help a stranger in distress if they were not in a hurry than if they were late for an appointment and therefore in a rush. (Sixty-three percent of students in the former situation helped, while only ten percent of students in the latter situation did.) While the presence or absence of time pressure determined whether a seminarian would stop and help, the students' own religious beliefs exerted no significant influence, nor did it matter much whether they had specifically been reminded of the helping behavior of the Good Samaritan just prior to encountering the hapless stranger. The students who were in a hurry and did not stop were not just being callous, however. In some cases those students moved on without helping simply because they did not have or take time to observe what was happening around them and therefore did not appreciate the victim's need for help. Some students actually stepped over the victim in their rush to get to their destination. In other cases, students in a hurry did not stop to help the victim because they felt a sense of obligation to get to the appointment for which they were running late and at which another person was depending on the student *to help him.*[12] (Conversely, it has been suggested that the students who were not in a hurry because they were running *early* for their appointments may have stopped in part because they were looking for a way to fill the time.)[13]

Another classic set of studies on helping behavior took as its inspiration the infamous Kitty Genovese case, in which a woman was stabbed repeatedly over a period of thirty minutes with at least thirty-eight people within earshot, none of whom came to her aid or even called the police. These studies also demonstrated the importance of situational variables—this time, the presence or absence of other bystanders. They showed that people were highly likely to help a stranger who was in danger if no other bystanders were available to help but were less and less likely to intervene as the number of other bystanders increased. The presence of other potential helpers is believed to channel unhelpful behavior in part because it dilutes or diffuses each person's sense of responsibility to help. An individual bystander might reason, for example, that someone else is likely to help or that others would be more competent to help. In addition, the inaction of others constructs the situation as one in which the victim's plight is not so serious and intervention would be both unwarranted and inappropriate.[14]

Harming behavior, too, can be greatly influenced by the situation. A well-known and disturbing set of eighteen studies by psychologist Stanley Milgram between 1960 and 1963 revealed the ease with which individuals can be manipulated to hurt others.[15] Milgram's studies showed the literally shocking lengths to which people of different ages and education levels and from different walks of life would go to knowingly harm others when the social context led them to feel that they had no choice but to do so—even when it should have been clear to them that they did. At the same time, however, the studies showed that the subjects' actions in inflicting harm were not consistent with their values, not expressions of aggression, nor even simply the consequence of their having especially weak characters. Instead, their actions were a product of the way the situation and their options for responding to it were presented to and perceived by the subjects. Here again, seemingly mild features of the situation played an important role in both defining the situation and signaling to the actor the appropriate course of conduct—or, to be more precise, in failing to provide the actor with a way "out" of harming another.

The basic experiment was presented to subjects as a study of the effect of punishment on memory and learning. Each subject was assigned, apparently randomly, the role of "teacher," in which he was to conduct a paired-associate word learning task that required responses of another volunteer, the "learner." Unbeknownst to the teacher-subject, the learner was in cahoots with the experimenters.

In a separate room from the teacher, the learner was strapped into an "electric chair" that appeared to be connected to a shock generator that the subject would control. The experimenter told the subject to give the learner a shock each time the learner gave a wrong answer and to increase the level of shock given with each wrong answer. The thirty lever switches on the shock generator had been marked with voltage designations (in increments of fifteen, from 15 to 450 volts) and with descriptive designations for groups of four switches, going from left to right and from lower to higher voltage levels: Slight Shock, Moderate Shock, Strong Shock, Very Strong Shock, Intense Shock, Extreme Intensity Shock, and Danger: Severe Shock. The two switches after that were simply labeled "XXX." Subjects were told that the shocks "could be extremely painful" but would "cause no permanent tissue damage." The switches and electric apparatus were, of course, all fake.

Milgram, other behavioral scientists, and lay people whom Milgram surveyed before he conducted the studies all had predicted that almost no one, including themselves, would apply the highest levels of shock. These respondents assumed that people generally do not wish to hurt others and are motivated by "empathy, compassion, and a sense of justice."[16] Further, they believed that individuals' actions are driven by their personal values and that they will not go against those values unless they are threatened or physically forced to do so.

What Milgram found when he put these assumptions to the test was startling. The learner, on cue, expressed discomfort at seventy-five volts, then, as the shock levels rose, protested verbally and increasingly vehemently, demanded to be released, eventually screamed in agony and pounded the wall with each shock, and finally stopped responding to the memory test and fell silent, even as he continued to "receive" shocks for failing to respond. Nevertheless, most subjects continued to raise the voltage to the highest level, frequently to their own psychological discomfort and even physical distress. Several subjects became so distraught that they began shaking, sweating, and stuttering, and some developed uncontrollable cases of nervous laughter. While many subjects expressed no verbal resistance to continuing the experiment, a number did state their reluctance to continue, protested against continuing the experiment, or denounced the exercise as "stupid and senseless." Surprisingly, however, few subjects—even among those who protested—actually terminated their participation. Most continued to the end without the application of any force or compulsion other than the experimenter's calm instructions, repeated as necessary, that they had no choice but to do so because the experiment required them to go on. In fact, all subjects should have known that they did have the choice whether or not to continue, for each knew that a failure to obey would result in no punishment—not even the loss of the fee the subject had been paid to participate.

What explains these breathtaking results? Milgram sought to answer that question by testing a series of small variations on the basic experimental setup—altering, for example, the institutional setting (changing it from the impressive environs of Yale University to the shabbier offices of a purportedly private research firm), the physical proximity of the learner or the experimenter to the subject, the number of teachers, the number of experimenters and their instructions to the subject, the choices of shock level available to the subject-teacher, and the role of the recipient of the shocks (having the subject administer shocks to an experimenter rather than to another lay volunteer). Some of these changes had no significant effect on subjects' obedience, while others produced significantly higher levels of disobedience.

Based on these results, Milgram ruled out the explanation that most closely conforms to "commonsense" interpretations of the behavior observed: that the subjects, taking advantage of a situation in which their conduct was socially acceptable, were acting out feelings of aggression, pent-up anger, or sadism. Milgram noted that, in experimental variations in which subjects did not receive unambiguous instructions to administer increasingly higher levels of shock or could get away without raising the level, they did not do so. He further pointed out that subjects in the other variations displayed a distaste toward their task, with many protesting it—all the while, however, complying with instructions to continue.

Instead, Milgram determined that *the social structure of the testing situation* played a critical role in channeling harming behavior *despite* the individual actors' wishes. People respond to socially determined definitions of a situation. The testing situation that subjects encountered was unfamiliar to them and, thus, subjects came to it without a stable "definition of the situation"—and with the events that ensued, the testing situation did not make sense to them. Therefore they were highly influenced by the definition provided by the experimenter, whom they identified as a legitimate authority figure. That authority prescribed the appropriate behavior for the situation. Further, with the authority directing the subjects to act in a particular way—though, again, with no real power to compel obedience—the subject's "moral focus" was not on the learner but on the authority's expectations of him, and so the subject assessed his performance according to how well he had carried out his duty to the authority. This sense of duty to authority, in turn, allowed the subject to separate his actions from his "self," and thereby to shift responsibility for those actions to the authority.

The sequential, incremental nature of the prescribed actions reinforced the subject's compliance, for as he continued to deliver increasingly painful shocks, the subject felt the need to justify what he had done. As Milgram explained, "one form of justification is to go to the end. For if he breaks off, he must say to himself: 'Everything I have done to this point is bad, and I now acknowledge it by breaking off.' But, if he goes on, he is reassured about his past performance."[17] Moreover, in order to end his pattern of conduct, the subject would have to breach the "situational etiquette" that the testing situation had established: "[T]he subject must breach the implicit set of understandings that are part of the social occasion. He made an initial promise to aid the experimenter, and now he must renege on this commitment."[18] To do so, the subject would have to violate the experimenter's definition of the situation and risk appearing "arrogant, untoward, and rude."[19] Milgram found that most people would prefer to continue inflicting severe pain on the learner than to contend with the awkwardness and embarrassment of disrupting the well-defined social situation.

Yet, changing even an apparently small feature of the testing situation produced dramatically different results—much more disobedience—if the change was one that either altered the definition of the situation or opened up a "disobedience channel." One way Milgram changed the situation was by making the learner more salient to the subject and the experimenter comparatively less so: in these variations, he moved the learner increasingly close to the subject; in some instances he required the subject to place his hand over the learner's. The closer proximity of the learner to the subjects produced significantly higher levels of disobedience because, in conjunction with making the victim more prominent to the subject and the authority less so, their closeness made clearer to the subject the connection between his actions and the victim's pain and allowed the subject to form an alliance with the victim rather than with the authority.

Altering the testing situation to undermine the stability of its authority-determined definition produced the same results. Milgram did this by conducting a variation in which, instead of facing one experimenter who conveyed unequivocally the appropriate behavior, the subject faced two experimenters who gave conflicting instructions on how to behave when he balked at continuing: one experimenter told him he must continue, while the other directed him to stop. The results of this conflict were dramatic; every subject abruptly ended the shocks at or near the point of the authorities' disagreement. Milgram explained that the contradictory instructions "paralyzed" the action—"stopped [it] dead in its tracks"—by destroying the hierarchical structure of the situation.[20] (Some subjects even tried to reconstruct the hierarchy by trying to determine which of the two experimenters was the higher authority.) Notably, this confusion produced an immediate end to the test, whereas in cases in which the authority's instructions were unequivocal, nothing the learner did, no matter how insistent his pleading or dire his apparent condition, was nearly as effective. Further, no subject in the conflicting authorities experiments took advantage of the justification for inflicting pain that the instruction to continue would have provided.

Offering the subject a "way out" of complying with instructions—especially a way to disobey without openly defying the authority's directive—also produced a high degree of disobedience.

Milgram created this condition by placing the experimenter in a remote location—a separate room—from which the subject perceived that the experimenter was unable to monitor the subject's actions. The experimenter still was able to communicate with the subject by telephone, giving the same instructions as in the basic experiment. This variation produced interesting results: first, a much higher number of subjects disobeyed the experimenter when he gave orders by telephone than when he was physically present. Second, several subjects kept up a pretense of following instructions—reporting in their phone conversations that they were raising the shock level as directed—while actually subverting the authority by giving the lowest shock available. Notably, the experimenter was able to restore obedience when he reappeared in the testing room.

Milgram's studies demonstrated the power of the social environment to induce individuals, contrary to their own values or wishes, to knowingly harm innocent people.[21] The studies suggest the potential, in particular, for authorities to induce subordinates to commit deeds of extraordinary evil and have been cited to explain the complicity of ordinary Germans in the atrocities of the Holocaust and the actions of American soldiers in torturing and massacring civilian villagers during the Vietnam War.[22] At a more general level, the studies illustrate the power of small, seemingly insignificant features of a situation to channel behavior in a dramatic direction and the error in trying to interpret individuals' actions without appreciating their understanding of the situation and the influence of social expectations on their perceptions of appropriate behavior.

These insights help us understand modern-day racial discrimination, marked as it is by an apparent mismatch between widely shared egalitarian values and subtle but pervasive racially discriminatory behavior. Of course, the reasons for the entrenchment of racial discrimination are numerous and complex, and they operate at the societal, institutional, social, and individual levels. But one factor that we may not appreciate is the power of the *situation* to channel discriminatory behavior even in those who do not realize that they are, and would not want to be, discriminating. In particular, social psychologists who study contemporary discrimination have discovered, much as Milgram did, the power of *ambiguity* or the lack of definitional clarity in a situation to open a channel to behavior that otherwise would seem clearly wrong. The situational ambiguity that promotes discrimination, moreover, also serves to mask it, by shifting the actor's "moral focus" and alleviating his sense of responsibility for his behavior, much as the social structure of Milgram's basic experimental setup supported the subjects' decisions to continue shocking their partners.

Normative Ambiguity and Modern Discrimination

The situations that might be expected to promote discrimination are not necessarily those in which it is most likely to occur. Nor are the situations in which discrimination is easy to see the ones in which it is likely to be found. One might assume that racial bias is most likely to come to the fore in situations in which racial issues are prominent, such as in a criminal trial when the prosecution or defense "plays the race card" by drawing attention to racial differences between the defendant and victim. For example, in a case in which the state charges a Black defendant with assaulting a White victim, one might expect that drawing attention to the defendant's race or presenting evidence of racial tensions between the parties would lead White jurors to judge the defendant more harshly than if those differences were downplayed. Such an expectation might have been warranted with respect to White juries of the past, when overtly racist norms were more acceptable than they are today. However, as explicit racial norms have changed, so have the situational factors that are likely to cue racially discriminatory decisions and behavior.

Social psychological research shows that, today, making racial issues *salient* rather than obscuring them can actually reduce the racial bias exhibited by Whites. Studies of White juror bias in mock trials, for example, have revealed that discrimination occurs less frequently when racial issues are highlighted than when they are downplayed. Those studies compared White subjects' decisions in cases of interracial crime involving Black or White defendants when racial issues were explicitly mentioned to decisions in cases involving the same facts but no mention of race-related issues. The subjects tended to judge Black defendants more harshly than Whites and also to view the evidence against Black defendants as stronger and their defenses as weaker when racial issues were not explicitly mentioned in the trial summary. When racial issues were explicitly raised, however, jurors reached comparable decisions for Black and White defendants.[23]

These results show that situations characterized by normative clarity—that is, situations that include clear indications of right and wrong behavior—tend to reduce the likelihood of discrimination. In particular, they suggest that in situations in which racial issues are conspicuous, people are mindful of their egalitarian ideals and are more likely to make an effort to avoid acting on racial prejudice. When racial issues are obscured, on the other hand, they often do not guard against, but instead act on, racial bias.[24]

While salience and clarity tend to reduce discrimination, "normative ambiguity" has been found to promote it—and, significantly, the power of ambiguity to channel discrimination goes hand in hand with its ability to mask it. Normative ambiguity can arise in a couple of different ways.[25] The situation may be one in which appropriate (and, accordingly, inappropriate) behavior is not clearly identified. Examples of this kind of ambiguous behavior might include hanging up on a caller who has dialed the wrong number rather than staying on the line and helping him get a message to its intended recipient, or walking past a shopper struggling with a broken shopping bag rather than stopping to help gather her fallen items.[26] In such a case, choosing to act indifferently or unhelpfully toward a Black person does not necessarily mark one as a racist because it is not clear that what one has done is wrong.

A situation may also be ambiguous if clearly negative behavior can be rationalized or justified on some basis other than race. For example, an employer or college admissions officer who rejects a Black applicant with "mixed" qualifications—some strong credentials and some weak—is not necessarily doing so for racist reasons, because the weaker elements of the candidate's record can support the negative decision.[27]

Social scientists have demonstrated the channeling power of both kinds of ambiguity in studies that included variations on the helping behavior studies discussed earlier. They have discovered that situational ambiguity creates an opening through which our biased expectations and attitudes—like Milgram's authority figure—can define the situation in a way that makes our negative treatment of others seem appropriate and even justified.

A number of experimental studies have confirmed the effect of the first type of situational ambiguity in promoting discrimination by White subjects. A fairly recent study found racially disparate responses when it tested simultaneously the effects of two different types of factors on helping behavior: the perceived *reason* why the victim needed help (that is, whether the victim was to blame for needing help because she did not try hard enough on an assigned task or whether, instead, an external factor had caused her problem) and the *source of the request* for help from the bystander (the victim herself or a third party). Discrimination against Black victims occurred in situations in which the victims both appeared to have caused their own problems and asked for help from the bystander. Conversely, Black victims were treated just as favorably as, or even more favorably than, Whites when bystanders perceived that the victims' plight was caused by factors outside their control (regardless of who asked for help) *or* when a third party requested that the bystander help (regardless of the cause of the victims' predicament). The researchers pointed out that, in this experiment, normative clarity discouraged racial bias but normative ambiguity channeled it: subjects chose to discriminate when they could rationalize a failure to help by viewing the help as "undeserved," but not when such a characterization was unwarranted or another party signaled that it was not appropriate to withhold assistance.[28]

Experiments have confirmed the discrimination-promoting effect of the second type of normative ambiguity, under which clearly negative behavior can be justified on some basis other than race. They have shown, moreover, that different rationales can be constructed to fit different situations.

Once again, researchers used a series of helping studies to test the responsiveness of White bystanders to the misfortunes of Black and White victims under various conditions and thereby to study the effect of nonracial justifications on spontaneous decision making. They found no discrimination in the simplest—and only normatively *un*ambiguous—scenario, involving one victim and one bystander-subject. In those situations, bystanders helped Black victims as often and readily as or more frequently and quickly than White victims. When researchers introduced complications that could form a nonracial basis for rationalizing a failure to help, however, the subjects did discriminate against Black victims, helping them significantly less frequently or less quickly than White victims.

First, in a study modeled closely on the classic bystander intervention studies discussed above, a bystander's awareness that others were nearby (though not immediately present), and the attendant diffusion of her sense of responsibility to help, put Black victims at a significant disadvantage compared to White victims: Black victims were helped only half as often as Whites, and when they did receive help it was significantly slower in coming.[29] A second study showed that White subjects were more susceptible to social pressure not to intervene when the victim was Black than when the victim was White. In that study, although almost all bystanders ultimately did help both Black and White victims, they were significantly slower to help Black than White victims if they were in the face-to-face presence of others who made no move to help.[30]

In addition to demonstrating the channeling effect of normative ambiguity, the studies also showed its flexibility, because the researchers determined that subjects in the two studies had constructed different rationalizations to suit their respective situations: whereas a diffused sense of responsibility channeled discrimination in the first study, social pressure to conform produced a similar effect in the second. Key differences in the design and results of the two studies supported these differing interpretations. First, subjects in the first study did not face social pressure because they were merely *told* that others were nearby, whereas subjects in the second study were in the immediate presence of the other bystanders. In addition, subjects in the first study who thought no one else was helping tended to justify their inaction in the belief that the victim's plight was not serious, whereas subjects in the second study did not evaluate the seriousness of the victim's situation any differently based on the presence of nonresponsive others. Finally, subjects in the first study had lower heart rates if others were available than if they were alone, a result that indicates they felt less responsible when others were nearby. Subjects in the second study, on the other hand, had *higher* heart rates if others were present than if they were alone. This heightened level of arousal in the presence of others suggested that subjects in the face-to-face presence of nonresponsive bystanders did not feel less responsible, but instead were contending with a dilemma—whether to help the victim or to conform to the behavior of the others. Their disparate responses showed that pressure to conform exerted a stronger influence on subjects when the victim was Black than when the victim was White.

Researchers observed similar channeling effects when they examined decision making by White subjects in more deliberative contexts, such as recommendations for employment or college admissions[31] and mock jury deliberations in criminal cases. The criminal studies are particularly illuminating. In these settings, subjects reached conclusions that were significantly harsher toward Black than White defendants—but, again, only when the decision was not likely to be seen as racist because a nonracial justification was available to support the negative decision.

For example, in a study of juror deliberations in the sentencing phase of a mock death penalty case in which all other jurors spoke in favor of death, "low-prejudice" jurors (those who had shown less unfavorable attitudes toward Blacks during a pretest than did "high prejudice" jurors) favored the death penalty more strongly for Black than for White defendants—*if* the otherwise all-White jury included one Black juror who advocated death. When the jury comprised solely White jurors, on the other hand, low-prejudice subjects did not discriminate against Black defendants, but instead treated them more favorably than White defendants.[32]

Subjects' responses to a postdeliberation questionnaire evaluating the other jurors eliminated a possible substantive basis for the effect of the Black juror's advocacy of death in the case of the Black defendant: namely, that subjects perceived the Black juror's views as being more credible and persuasive because he stated a position that was against the interests of his own racial group. Instead, the disparate outcomes appeared to result from subjects' ability to avoid an attribution of racial bias in their decisions favoring death when a Black juror also advocated death. In other words, the Black juror's advocacy seems to have provided "cover" for the subject on that score.

Similarly, the availability of a nonracial justification increased discrimination against Black defendants in a study examining the influence of race on the use of inadmissible evidence of guilt in reaching a verdict. In that study, jurors reached similar verdicts for Black and White defendants when the evidence at issue was either omitted (the "control" condition) or admissible. However, results differed significantly when subjects were presented with the evidence of guilt but later told to disregard it because it had been ruled inadmissible. Subjects reached significantly harsher verdicts for Black than for White defendants in that condition. Further, when compared with verdicts reached in the control condition, the effect on jurors' verdicts of the inadmissible evidence was significantly greater for Black than for White defendants.[33]

Paradoxically, jurors *perceived* themselves as being significantly *less* influenced by the inadmissible evidence in cases involving Black defendants than in those involving Whites. The researchers explained the greater influence of inadmissible evidence on decisions involving Black defendants as likely being the result of subjects' rationalizing their verdicts as not being racist but instead as decisions to do "the right thing" by not permitting a guilty person to go free. The researchers also speculated that the subjects' perception that they were less influenced by inadmissible evidence of Black defendants' guilt was a reflection of the subjects' predisposition to believe that Black defendants were guilty.[34]

Perhaps the most interesting point to emerge from the studies of both spontaneous and deliberative decision making is the researchers' explanation of *why* the existence of a justification for a negative decision disadvantaged Black victims and defendants to a greater degree than it did Whites. The nonracial justification for a negative decision—that is, the factor that made each situation normatively ambiguous—could have supported equally negative decisions for White victims and defendants as for Blacks. However, the racially disparate results in each study showed that such factors were *more powerful* when subjects had to make decisions affecting Blacks than when their decisions affected Whites. In other words, in addition to introducing ambiguity into the situation, *the nonracial justification became more salient and potent when it supported the negative treatment of Blacks.*[35]

Situational Racists

At least three explanations might account for the power of ambiguous situations to channel discrimination or, more generally, for the seeming mismatch between attitudes and actions that emerges in such situations. First, the mismatch may be more apparent than real: discrimination in ambiguous situations might actually provide a truer indication of an individual's beliefs than does his behavior in normatively clear contexts, when he would avoid discriminating in order to present and preserve a nonracist public image. This actor takes advantage of ambiguous situations to engage in "impression management."[36] That is, he was simply looking for an excuse or opportunity to discriminate that would allow him to indulge his "taste for discrimination" while appearing to conform to popular social norms.

Alternatively, the mismatch between attitudes and actions may indeed be real, at least at some level—the result of a genuine conflict between an individual's sincere egalitarian ideals and his unacknowledged, largely unconscious, negative feelings toward and beliefs about Blacks. The desire to maintain an egalitarian *self*-image might prevent him from discriminating in situations when it clearly would be inappropriate, but his hidden negative feelings prompt him to discriminate in "subtle, indirect, and rationalizable ways"—that is, by ambiguous means or in ambiguous situations—because he can do so without seeing himself as racist. In this case, the actor most likely does not intend to discriminate and is fooling himself as much as he fools others in striving to maintain a nonracist self-image.[37]

Finally, the explanation might lie not in the actor's racist *feelings* or *beliefs*, but in her unconscious *cognitive* biases. This account would distinguish between an actor's personal beliefs and values, which direct her conscious decisions of how to behave, and her unconsciously held stereotypes, which she absorbed from childhood, which are constantly being reinforced through social and cultural influences, and which, like a "bad habit," direct her behavior when she is not consciously monitoring it. When normative clarity cues the need to be mindful—and assuming she has the requisite "intention, attention, and time"[38]—an individual can control her response and act in a nonprejudiced way that is consistent with her nonracist beliefs. However, she is likely to discriminate in ambiguous situations despite her egalitarian values and lack of prejudice, because she may not be aware of the need to monitor her response and because racial stereotypes are always accessible and automatically activated, and will lead her to discriminate despite her best intentions.[39]

Of these three explanations, only the first conforms to the conventional discrimination schema and might result in liability under the traditional intent requirement. The other two explanations, on the other hand, are more likely to capture most contemporary discrimination. Certainly, old-fashioned discrimination still exists. Social psychologists who have studied racism and other forms of prejudice, however, believe that hard-core, committed bigots comprise a much smaller share of the population than in the past. Today, more people seem to embrace egalitarian values and to truly want to treat others fairly. Certainly, they want to *see* themselves as the kind of people who would not discriminate. Most people probably do not realize the extent to which they do discriminate, however, because they are acting on unconscious biases—whether cognitive (race and other group-based stereotypes), motivational (the desire to maintain and promote the interests of their own group), sociocultural (internalized societal values, beliefs, and traditions), or a combination thereof.[40]

Modern Discrimination's Challenge to the Legal Model

Whatever the underlying basis for the power of situational ambiguity to channel discrimination, the point remains that the situations that are most likely to lead to discrimination are also those that tend to mask it, making the legal question of whether the actor intended to discriminate—that is, whether race was the "real" reason for her decision—both difficult to answer and unlikely to arise.

The normative ambiguity studies show that racially biased treatment and legitimate, nondiscriminatory justifications are likely to coexist in many cases. More specifically, they show that the existence of a legitimate justification for a negative decision does not necessarily discredit racial bias as an explanation for that decision. The presence of such a justification may, instead, be cause to suspect that the decision in fact was racially biased, because racial discrimination today seems most likely to occur through the *racially biased application* of a *nondiscriminatory reason*.

This likelihood presents two significant challenges to the use of traditional, individual adjudication as a means of redressing discrimination. First, it suggests that discrimination can easily occur in individual cases without being detected, because the existence of a legitimate reason can mask the fact that the neutral reason was applied in a racially biased manner. In the experiments discussed, the researchers themselves were able to identify the racially discriminatory effect of nondiscriminatory justifications because they replicated the same situation numerous times and could see the pattern that emerged when the cases were viewed in the aggregate. Rarely in life will the same situation be repeated with nothing changed but the races of the targets, in this fashion. As a result, even the victims of discrimination may not realize what has happened, many cases of discrimination are likely to escape notice, and a large share of modern discrimination is likely to go unremedied.

Second, the studies cast doubt on the intentional discrimination model's assumption that the unlawful, discriminatory reason can be disentangled from the lawful, nondiscriminatory reason that could support the same conclusion.[41] The intentional discrimination model requires the fact finder to engage in an exercise in causal attribution[42]—to answer the question, "Why did the defendant treat the plaintiff negatively?"—by making a choice between alternative accounts: did the plaintiff's race affect the decision, as she alleges, or was it, as the defendant claims, based entirely on some legitimate, nondiscriminatory reason? Did the employer fail to hire the candidate because of her race or because another candidate was better qualified? Did the police officer stop the driver because of his race or because he committed a minor traffic violation?

The prevailing legal model of discrimination—the intentional discrimination model—only "knows how to tell" these two stories.[43] In the employment setting, for example, even the two disparate treatment doctrines that would seem to recognize that discriminatory and nondiscriminatory justifications can appear in the same case—the pretext and mixed-motive doctrines—ultimately require the fact finder to make a choice between two competing explanations. Under pretext doctrine, "it is simply not possible for an employment decision to be both motivated by the employer's articulated reasons *and* tainted by intergroup bias; the trier of fact must decide between the two."[44] Mixed-motives doctrine, too, assumes that the fact finder can determine whether the same decision would have been made for a legitimate reason wholly without regard to the plaintiff's race, because it assumes that the decision maker himself is sufficiently self-aware that he drew that distinction when he made the crucial decision.[45]

The law concerning racial profiling in law enforcement also reflects this dichotomous view of decision making. Legal scholars have pointed out that it is easy for a police officer to find a legitimate reason to stop almost any driver, because "no one can drive for even a few blocks without committing a minor violation—speeding, failing to signal or make a complete stop, touching a lane or center line, or driving with a defective piece of vehicle equipment."[46] Yet in this area as well, the relevant jurisprudence divides the world into "two neat, straightforward categories: those in which there clearly is and those in which there clearly is not 'probable cause'" for a stop.[47]

Under current Fourth Amendment law, as announced in the U.S. Supreme Court's 1996 decision *Whren v. United States*, a police officer's subjective use of race in deciding to make a traffic stop will not invalidate that stop if an objectively valid reason *could have* supported the decision. As the Court explained in *Whren*, it "[has] never held . . . that an officer's motive invalidates objectively justifiable behavior under the Fourth Amendment; but . . . [has] repeatedly held and asserted the contrary. . . . Subjective intentions play no role in ordinary, probable-cause Fourth Amendment analysis."[48] (The Court has instead relegated claims of racial discrimination in law enforcement to the equal protection clause and its discriminatory purpose doctrine.)[49] As a result, the Supreme Court's decisions

> treat race as a subject that can be antiseptically removed from a suppression hearing judge's review of whether a police officer had

> probable cause for an arrest or warrantless search or reasonable suspicion for a stop or frisk. The decisions imagine a world in which some officers are wholly unaffected by racial considerations and in which even biased officers may make objectively valid judgments that courts can sustain despite the underlying racial motivations of the officer.[50]

As several legal scholars have explained, this decision invites officers to invent race-neutral, pretextual reasons for making discriminatory stops, for they have been reassured that courts will not look beyond the proffered reason for the stop. Yet even the pretextual reasons that are offered might incorporate racially biased reasoning, for seemingly race-neutral reasons often are accepted because their believability correlates with the race of the suspect. That is, the myth that certain social groups are especially prone to criminal or deviant behavior makes seemingly race-neutral reasons more believable and allows for the apparent separation of racial bias and reasonable suspicion or probable cause. As David Cole has stated, "The Court's removal of meaningful Fourth Amendment review allows the police to rely on unparticularized discretion, unsubstantiated hunches, and nonindividualized suspicion. Racial prejudice and stereotypes linking racial minorities to crime rush to fill the void."[51]

Moreover, some officers who make racially biased decisions may not even intend to discriminate. Law enforcement officers, like everyone else, are likely to have incorporated racial stereotypes into their perceptions and understandings of the world. Among these stereotypes are the assumptions that people of color are especially prone to deviant or criminal behavior. When officers are called on to make complicated and grave decisions under stressful, time-pressured conditions, they are likely to rely on these stereotypes in interpreting the behavior of others. As a result, behavior that might appear harmless in a White person may seem criminal or threatening in a Black person, and the officer may "see" probable cause or reasonable grounds to be suspicious of the Black person.[52]

While the law requires the fact finder to select a decisive reason for the defendant's decision, the truth may be that the two possibilities—race and some other reason—are not really distinct. To be more precise, the truth may be that the decision maker relied on the nondiscriminatory reason in making her decision but saw that reason as persuasive only because of the plaintiff's race.

Meeting the Challenge

Far from being solely the product of an actor's conscious desire and preference to discriminate, discrimination can occur when the actor is unaware that his actions are biased, and largely *because* he is unaware of the potential for bias. Discrimination, in other words, can easily occur by default.

Once we realize that discrimination can occur by default, we also should recognize the hope that we can override the default. That is, at the same time as it reveals the difficulty of determining why, and even whether, an individual has discriminated in a particular case, our realization of the power of the situation to channel discrimination should give us hope for change, because situations are not purely "given." They can be altered in ways that reduce the potential for normative ambiguity and hence for subtle and rationalizable, but nonetheless real, discrimination to occur.

Before we can override the default setting by altering those situations, however, we must first recognize the role that each of us plays in *creating* the situations that channel discrimination. Individuals can, and often do, actively construct normatively ambiguous, discrimination-promoting situations, whether or not we realize that we are doing so. In particular, we sometimes act on group-based stereotypes in a way that generates the apparently neutral justifications that both promote and justify discrimination. As we shall see, moreover, the real power of biased expectations lies not just in their ability to create ambiguous situations and channel discriminatory behavior, but in their ability to do so while concealing their own influence.

3

Self-Fulfilling Stereotypes

Almost twenty years ago, when I was a young lawyer working at a large firm in a big city, I had an experience that has remained vivid in my memory. It was a moment of little consequence but with, I think, large implications.

I was sitting in the office of my gynecologist, shortly after he had found a sizable lump on my ovary and examined it through an ultrasound. Although he clearly was alarmed by this discovery, the doctor calmly listed the steps I needed to take over the next few days in preparation for surgery to remove the lump the following week: talk with my husband and parents about the surgery, inform my law firm that I needed to take at least six weeks of leave, come back to the hospital for presurgical tests, and so on. I listened carefully to his instructions, wrote down the relevant dates, took the pages of medical information he handed me, and prepared to leave his office. But the doctor did not excuse me even after I had finished taking notes and indicated that I understood what I had to do. Instead, he continued to gaze at me intently, making no move to get up from his chair. I was both puzzled by his behavior and impatient to get going. Gradually, I began to realize that the doctor was not satisfied with my response. "Oh," I thought, "he expects me to cry." To fulfill what I assumed to be his expectation and get his permission to leave, I complied, producing a small but convincing amount of tears. Apparently satisfied, the doctor nodded his head and showed me to the door.

This is how I analyze that experience: because of my youth, the doctor worried that I would not understand the potential seriousness of my situation. Because of my gender, he expected that I would indicate my understanding by becoming emotional—specifically, by crying. However, I tend to be fairly optimistic and stoic about health-related matters. I did understand the seriousness of the lump: I might have had ovarian cancer. I did not, on the other hand, think it likely that I had cancer (as it turned out, I did not), and in any event did not feel especially emotional about the possibility. But most immediately, I wanted to get back to work and then home so I could tell the appropriate parties about my plans for the coming weeks. So I produced the tears that turned out to be my ticket out of the doctor's office. In the process, I likely confirmed my doctor's assumption that women cry when they get bad news.

I learned in that doctor's office about the power of expectations. We often are motivated, as I was that day, by a conscious desire to meet other people's, or our own, expectations. But even when—and perhaps especially when—we are not conscious of them, expectations exert a control over our perceptions and actions. Expectations can trick us, leading us to see something that isn't there. As the tragic killing of Amadou Diallo and several experimental studies demonstrate, in a tense moment we might see a gun in the hand of a Black man who is really holding a wallet.[1] Expectations can skew the way we see the world, other people, and ourselves, molding our interpretations of events and conduct to conform to them. Until symphony orchestras began holding "blind" auditions with musicians performing behind a screen or curtain, they tended almost exclusively to hire male musicians; since the advent of blind auditions, the gender balance in symphony orchestras has evened out significantly. In the past, it seems, conductors, music directors, and maestros expected male musicians to sound better than females—*and they did*, at least when their gender was apparent.[2]

Expectations wield their power whether they are right or wrong, but we may never learn that they were wrong because sometimes they can exert their influence without leaving a trace. In other words, and as this chapter will show, expectations have the power to produce concrete, objective evidence to support their own validity even if they are wholly without merit. In illuminating the process by which expectations can be falsely verified, this chapter provides another account of how discriminatory patterns of interaction are reinforced, by showing how expectations of a particularly harmful kind—group-based stereotypes—can be "confirmed" and strengthened despite their inaccuracy.

The phenomenon that produces these results is the "self-fulfilling prophecy": a process by which people, acting on the basis of an assumption or prediction, and regardless of its truth or falsity, actually cause that assumption to be verified or the prediction to occur, thereby confirming the "accuracy" of the belief. This process in social interactions is simply one variation of a long recognized, though continually surprising, phenomenon by which expectations influence and then become "reality." In an influential 1948 essay, sociologist Robert K. Merton pointed out the resiliency and power of this "basic process of society" when he wrote that "[t]he specious validity of the self-fulfilling prophecy perpetuates a reign of error. For the prophet will cite the actual course of events as proof that he was right from the very beginning. . . . Such are the perversities of social logic."[3]

The self-fulfilling prophecy is a familiar phenomenon. A typical scenario occurs when an individual who expects to do well or poorly at a task (for example, an athletic feat) ends up performing at the predicted level. Frustrated market watchers will recognize the common pattern in which predictions of a sluggish economy lead consumers and investors to reduce their spending and investing, thereby causing the economy actually to slow down in confirmation of the prediction. Another example is the California gas "shortage" of 1979, when newspapers' predictions of an impending gasoline shortage caused motorists to fill up their gas tanks and to keep them full, which surge in demand exhausted the reserves and "so brought about the predicted shortage practically overnight. . . . After the excitement died down, it turned out that the allotment of gasoline to the state of California had hardly been reduced at all."[4] Our beliefs about other people can set in motion a similar process.

Stereotypes as Channel Factors

The idea that "expectations have consequences because they exist, regardless of whether they are accurate or inaccurate"[5] has significant implications for the perpetuation of the biased treatment of certain groups. Because group-based stereotypes and prejudice are simply expectations about people, they too can be "confirmed" through a self-fulfilling process. Merton declared in 1948 that "[i]t is the self-fulfilling prophecy which goes far toward explaining the dynamics of ethnic and racial conflict in the America of today."[6] Both historically and in contemporary times, the self-fulfilling effect of negative group-based expectancies has operated at many levels—in societal structures, public policies, social interaction, and even within the stereotyped individual himself or herself—to provide putative justification for the biased treatment of disfavored social groups. As a result, stereotypes act not only as erroneous judgments of those groups but also lead to the production of objective facts to support their own accuracy.

At the highest of these levels, institutional structures in society that incorporate stereotypes have contributed to the false "confirmation" of those stereotypes. As social psychologist Richard D. Ashmore pointed out in 1970,

> At a societal level, the self-fulfilling prophecy works by creating a political, economic, and social structure which dooms outgroup members to an inferior position. This structure in America has aptly been called institutional racism. . . . For example, in the days of slavery black people were regarded as intellectually inferior and consequently were seldom taught to read and write. Without education, the slaves were indeed less intellectually sophisticated than the masters. In short, the stereotype of the black person led to dis-

> criminatory practices which produced black people congruent with that stereotype.[7]

Contemporary policies and practices based on social group stereotypes also generate their own statistical justification through their very enforcement. Legal scholars have identified this phenomenon in the use of racial profiling in policing. David Harris, for example, has written:

> [T]he belief that blacks are disproportionately involved in drug crimes will become a self-fulfilling prophecy: Because police will look for drug crime among black drivers, they will find it disproportionately among black drivers. More blacks will be arrested, prosecuted, convicted, and jailed, thereby reinforcing the idea that blacks constitute the majority of drug offenders. This will provide a continuing motive and justification for stopping more black drivers as a rational way of using resources to catch the most criminals. At the same time, because police will focus on black drivers, white drivers will receive less attention, and the drug dealers and possessors among them will be apprehended in proportionately smaller numbers than their presence in the population would predict.[8]

Similarly, Chief Justice William Rehnquist recently described the subtle way in which the stereotype of women as caregivers is perpetuated through employment practices that rest on, reinforce, and obscure the discriminatory stereotype:

> Stereotypes about women's domestic roles are reinforced by parallel stereotypes presuming a lack of domestic responsibilities for men. Because employers continued to regard the family as the woman's domain, they often denied men similar accommodations or discouraged them from taking leave. These mutually reinforcing stereotypes created a self-fulfilling cycle of discrimination that forced women to continue to assume the role of primary family caregiver, and fostered employers' stereotypical views about

> women's commitment to work and their value as employees. Those perceptions, in turn, . . . lead to subtle discrimination that may be difficult to detect on a case-by-case basis.[9]

(Conversely, in-group favoritism can produce its own justifications as well: in an employment setting, for example, an in-group member who has "profited over time from a series of subtle, incremental advantages is apt to be objectively better situated" than out-group members who have not so profited when the time comes for a hiring or promotion decision to be made.)[10]

Moreover, members of stigmatized groups themselves may be vulnerable to negative expectations of their group—and, ironically, the very fear of serving as a source of confirmation of those expectations may *cause* group members to perform consistently with expectations. In a series of experiments, social psychologists Joshua Aronson, Claude Steele, and their colleagues have documented a phenomenon they call "stereotype threat."[11] This process causes members of groups that are stereotyped as being less able intellectually—particularly those individuals who care the most about their intellectual performance—to perform more poorly on standardized tests when that stereotype is made salient to them than when the stereotype is not invoked. Specifically, the researchers found that African American, Latino, and female students performed significantly worse than Caucasian male students on standardized tests in areas such as verbal or math ability in which their group is stereotyped as having lesser ability—but *only* when they were tested after somehow being "reminded" of the negative stereotype (by, for example, being asked to indicate their race on a questionnaire before taking the test). When researchers did not induce stereotype threat, the members of these groups performed just as well as White male subjects on the relevant tests.

The effects of stereotype threat extend beyond race and gender and beyond performance on tests of academic ability. In subsequent experiments by other researchers, stereotype threat impaired performance of a variety of tasks by members of other groups who are vulnerable to negative stereotypes about their abilities. In one study, subjects of lower socioeconomic status did worse on a verbal test when they were reminded of the stereotype linking low socioeconomic status to low intellectual ability and better when they were not,[12] and in another, adults between the ages of 62 and 84 did worse on tests of recall when they were reminded of the stereotype linking age with memory decline and better when they were not.[13] Athletic performance, too, is susceptible to the influence of stereotype threat. In a pair of studies, Black and White athletes both performed worse on a test of athletic skill when the test was framed in terms of a negative stereotype that applied to their own racial group than when that stereotype was not made salient. To induce stereotype threat, researchers told Black athletes the test measured "sports intelligence"—a phrase used to trigger the stereotype that Black athletes are intellectually inferior (albeit physically superior)—while they told White athletes the test measured "natural athletic ability," a reminder that White athletes are stereotyped as physically inferior, if intellectually superior.[14]

Steele and Aronson have described stereotype threat as a *situational factor* based in "domain identification." That is, when an individual from a stereotyped group cares enough about the ability supposedly being measured to want the stereotype of low ability to be untrue, the test becomes a "high-stakes endeavor." The individual then feels apprehensive, anxious, and distracted—emotions that interfere with performance on the test. In other words, even when an individual's abilities do not conform to the stereotype—and especially when he or she wants to prove that the stereotype is invalid—making the stereotype salient alters the testing situation by placing an extra psychological burden on the individual. As the researchers explained, "The predicament is this: the mere existence of a devaluing stereotype means that anything one does, or any of one's features that conform to it, makes the stereotype more plausible as a self-characterization, in the eyes of others, and perhaps even in one's own eyes."[15] Over time, if exposure to stereotype threat is chronic, an individual may respond by "disidentifying" from the relevant domain—that is, by reconceptualizing herself so as "not [to care] about the domain in relation to the self." This response can also serve to "confirm" the stereotype.[16]

Because stereotype threat is a feature of the situation, the psychological burden of stereotype vulnerability is not unique to members of stigmatized groups but can affect anyone under the right circumstances. The experiment involving White athletes, described above, supports this situational conception of stereotype threat, as does an experiment in which Steele and Aronson tested the effect of stereotype threat on the math performance of White male students who, presumably, were not subject to any negative stereotypes about math ability. The researchers found that students who had previously identified themselves as caring about their math abilities performed significantly worse than students who did not so identify—but only when they were reminded of the stereotype that Asian students consistently outperform other groups on standardized tests of math ability. From this experiment, the researchers concluded that "one need not be a minority to be bothered by stereotypes," and that underperformance in this situation apparently results from "trying too hard."[17]

A converse self-fulfilling effect—stereotype *lift*—can work to "boost" the performance of group members in situations where they are not subject to negative stereotypes. A meta analysis of stereotype threat studies has shown that men and Whites receive a performance boost when they are reminded (whether explicitly or implicitly) of the negative stereotypes associated with other social groups before taking evaluative tests. The study's authors explain stereotype lift as the result of "downward social comparisons with a denigrated outgroup" that elevate the in-group member's "self-efficacy or sense of personal worth" and enhance performance by contributing to the individual's confidence and motivation. The authors view stereotype lift as complementary to stereotype threat and note its significant implications: "[A]lthough the effects of stereotype lift may be subtle on any given test, its impact on the achievement of the nonstereotyped may be dramatic when its effects accumulate either within a large group of test-takers or across numerous performance opportunities for a single individual."[18]

These examples demonstrate that stereotypes constitute more than just inaccurate overgeneralizations about groups of individuals. Stereotypes also operate as *channel factors*—they define situations in a way that limits the potential outcomes by directing a particular path for performance or behavior. As Merton said of self-fulfilling prophecies generally, "public definitions of a situation (prophecies or predictions) become an integral part of the situation and thus affect subsequent developments."[19]

Moreover, the real power of stereotypes as self-fulfilling prophecies lies in the failure of people to recognize the situation-defining role they play, and their tendency instead to see the outcome of the situation as objective evidence of the truth of (or "kernel of truth" in) the stereotype. As Merton put it:

> As a result of their failure to comprehend the operation of the self-fulfilling prophecy, many Americans of good will are (sometimes reluctantly) brought to retain enduring ethnic and racial prejudices. They experience these beliefs, not as prejudices, not as prejudgments, but as irresistible products of their own observation. "The facts of the case" permit them no other conclusion.[20]

This failure is simply another example of the correspondence bias or fundamental attribution error that, as we saw in chapter 2, leads people to attribute an individual's behavior solely to his or her disposition or personal qualities, and prevents them from seeing that the individual's behavior was also influenced by the situation. In the case of stereotypes, observers fail to recognize that a stereotyped individual's options are often limited by biased institutions or policies, or even simply by his awareness of others' stereotyped view of him. Instead, they think it obvious that the person's stereotype-consistent actions are an accurate reflection of who he "is," and the stereotype is therefore ascribed a validity that it does not merit.

Behavioral Confirmation of Stereotypes in Social Interaction

Self-fulfilling prophecies can operate to "confirm" and reinforce stereotypes—along with a host of other kinds of expectations—in social interactions as well. My experience at the doctor's office was hardly unusual. I imagine we all have stories of times when we felt that another person approached us with an erroneous expectation that we then supported through our own behavior, willingly or not. We all likely have been on the other side too, when we formed an impression of someone else—maybe because of something a third person said about him, the way he dressed, or who his friends were—and had that impression confirmed through our first interactions with him, only to learn after longer experience that we had misjudged him.

Again, the fundamental attribution error plays a critical role in promoting this self-fulfilling process, because when we observe other people, and when they observe us, we all tend to overlook the part that our own behavior played in eliciting one another's responses. Others who observe our interactions will judge our characters based on our actions as well, similarly overlooking the ways in which each person's behavior was affected by the constraints imposed by each of us on the other.

The behavioral confirmation of expectations in social interactions is a well-established phenomenon. In one famous experiment, for example, Robert Rosenthal and Lenore Jacobson found that when teachers were told that certain students (actually selected by the researchers at random) had the potential to achieve greater intellectual development, those children actually did show greater intellectual development later in the school year. The researchers believe that the teachers acted differently toward the identified students, using different teaching techniques and behaving in a way that communicated their high expectations. In turn, the teachers' behavior contributed to changes in the children's self-concepts, expectations, and motivation, and even the children's cognitive skills.[21] In short, "teachers teach more and teach it more warmly to students for whom they have more favorable expectations."[22] This "Pygmalion effect" can also operate among adults in the workplace, where supervisors' experimenter-induced expectations of high performance from designated workers have resulted in confirmation by supervisors' evaluations, peers' ratings, and objective tests of subjects' performance.[23]

Furthermore, expectations are contagious—a quality that magnifies their power by spreading their effects to third parties. For example, studies have found that judges may, through their nonverbal behavior, unwittingly convey to juries their beliefs about the guilt or innocence of a defendant.[24] When delivering jury instructions, judges who expected the defendant to be found guilty came across as "less warm, less competent, less wise, and more anxious"[25] than judges who expected a not guilty verdict. Another study found that when several individuals worked together on a task, team members unconsciously communicated to one another—by frowning, tightening their mouths, or furrowing their brows—their disapproval of female members who took assertive, leadership roles.[26] Jurors in the criminal cases and team members in the group tasks picked up these cues and themselves tended to perceive the defendant as guilty or the woman's contribution as less valuable.[27]

Collectively, these studies show the potential for expectations, whether accurate or not, to influence people's opportunities and outcomes in critical situations. As social psychologist Steven L. Neuberg has explained:

> [E]ach day, the outcomes of social encounters determine friendship choices, educational opportunities, job hirings, housing decisions, the ability of people to get along peacefully with each other, and so forth. When stereotypes and prejudices color such encounters, leading people to form mistaken impressions of others, the personal consequences of these encounters can be momentous for all parties involved.[28]

The Process of Behavioral Confirmation: The Studies

A number of social psychological experiments have demonstrated the channeling power of erroneous or constructed expectations in social interactions. In these experiments, individuals' expectations of others—that the other was hostile, extroverted, sociable, or even guilty of a crime—actually induced those others to behave in conformity with these expectations, thereby "confirming" them, even when the expectations were wholly created by the experimenters.[29] The experiments have further shown that this behavioral confirmation process is reciprocal, as both perceiver and target act in accordance with the perceiver's expectations and the corresponding signals that the perceiver's behavior sends to the target. Indeed, the falsely perceived individual may even come to see herself, or continue to behave, consistently with the perceiver's originally erroneous belief.[30]

Group-based stereotypes can also act as powerful channel factors in one-on-one interactions, especially between individuals who do not have prior experience with one another and therefore must make judgments on the basis of first impressions that are influenced strongly by the other person's most visible characteristics such as race, color, gender, age, or physical appearance. In these situations, we can expect that the initial impressions of people who have had no opportunity to learn about one another will incorporate general stereotypes that may lead to a grossly inaccurate impression of a particular individual. Further, cognitive biases often contribute to "perceptual confirmation" of the erroneous prejudgment, because people tend to "see" what they expect to see.[31] What is surprising, however, is that rather than disconfirming the perceiver's erroneous impression, the stereotyped individual's own behavior during the interaction often serves to confirm and strengthen the inaccurate expectation.

Two classic studies in the 1970s demonstrated the power of stereotypes to act as self-fulfilling prophecies and illuminated the interactive process by which behavioral confirmation of stereotypes occurs.

How Beautiful People Become Good People

Good-looking people seem to have it made. Not only do other people prefer to *look at* those who are physically attractive, but they may *like* physically attractive people more than others as well. Sometimes we are so dazzled by another person's appearance and image that we miss some serious failings. In committing what Malcolm Gladwell calls the "Warren Harding error," for example, Americans were so taken with the tall, handsome, presidential-looking Warren Harding that they elected a man who "was, most historians agree, one of the worst presidents in American history."[32]

Why do beautiful people have such an advantage? Could it be that they are, in fact, simply nicer than other people? Or does our thinking they are make it so?

In 1977, Mark Snyder, Elizabeth Decker Tanke, and Ellen Berscheid examined the effect of the stereotype that physically attractive people are more friendly and likable and found that this expectation creates its own behavioral confirmation.[33] To do so, the researchers set up a controlled "getting acquainted" telephone interaction between a male perceiver and a female target who did not know one another. Before the telephone conversation they gave each perceiver a photograph that he was told depicted his female interaction partner but that actually did not. (The female participants were not told of these photographs, nor did they receive photos of their male partners.) The photos had been prepared in advance and depicted the target as either physically attractive or physically unattractive. (The photos had been rated earlier by a different group of men.) A photo was assigned randomly to each set of partners, who did not otherwise see one another. They engaged in an unstructured, ten-minute telephone conversation, each side of which was tape recorded separately. Afterward, judges listened to separate tapes of either the perceiver's or the target's side of the conversations and assessed the participants' behavior.

The judges, who were completely unaware of the perceived attractiveness of the female targets, assessed those targets who had been randomly assigned to the "attractive" condition consistently with the stereotypical expectations. Specifically, they found them to "manifest greater confidence, greater animation, greater enjoyment of the conversation, and greater liking for their partners than those women who interacted with men who perceived them as physically unattractive."[34] As Snyder and his colleagues put it, "the 'beautiful' people became 'good' people."[35]

Just *how* did the "'beautiful' people" become "'good' people"? The study demonstrated that one reason why stereotypes are so resilient lies in their power to shape the context in which individuals get to know one another: stereotypes act as situational factors that channel behavior and thereby define the terms of the parties' interaction. By examining the judges' ratings of each participant's voice during the conversation, the researchers learned that both parties play a role in the behavioral confirmation process.

First, the researchers had clear evidence that the male perceivers formed their first impressions of the female targets based on the stereotype linking physical attractiveness with socially desirable personality traits, because each perceiver had been asked to characterize his initial impression of the target after seeing "her" photograph but before engaging in the telephone conversation. Perceivers who had been assigned "attractive" targets said that they expected their partners to be "comparatively sociable, poised, humorous, and socially adept," while those who had been assigned "unattractive" targets anticipated their partners would be "rather unsociable, awkward, serious, and socially inept."[36]

Second, the researchers found that these expectations set off a "chain of events" that led to the confirmation of the perceivers' artificially created expectations. The judges' ratings of the male perceivers' parts of the conversations indicated that the perceivers interacted differently with targets who had been assigned to different attractiveness conditions. Those perceivers who conversed with "attractive" targets presented *themselves* as "more sociable, sexually warm, interesting, independent, sexually permissive, bold, outgoing, humorous, obvious, and socially adept" than those men who spoke with "unattractive" partners.[37] The judges also assessed the perceivers in the attractive target condition as being more animated, confident, and comfortable in their conversations, and judged them as both *seeing* their partners and *being seen by* their partners as more attractive.

In turn, the targets responded consistently with the way they were being treated, so that those who *were believed to be* physically attractive, and therefore more likable, "actually *came to behave* in a friendly, likable, and sociable manner."[38] Thus, the perceivers' stereotypical but possibly erroneous expectations were realized.

Having witnessed the power of stereotypes to constrain targets' behavioral options and to elicit stereotype-consistent behavior, Snyder and his colleagues wondered about the larger societal implications of their findings: "Might not other important and widespread social stereotypes—particularly those concerning sex, race, social class, and ethnicity—also channel social interaction in ways that create their own social reality?" The researchers further speculated that "[a]ny self-fulfilling influences of social stereotypes may have compelling and pervasive societal consequences."[39]

The "Problem" of Black Performance

Indeed, in a slightly earlier study, Carl O. Word, Mark P. Zanna, and Joel Cooper had found that a self-fulfilling prophecy did operate in interracial encounters and in a setting that could have wide-ranging implications for an important social issue—Black unemployment.[40] Word and his colleagues conducted two related experiments to examine whether poor performances by Black persons in job interviews might sometimes be the result of a self-fulfilling prophecy by which a White interviewer's negative attitude toward a Black applicant elicited a less favorable performance from the applicant. Specifically, they hypothesized that a White interviewer might convey negative evaluations toward Blacks through nonverbal behavior and that a Black interviewee might reciprocate these nonverbal cues in a way that resulted in a negative assessment of the interview performance—thus confirming the interviewer's initial expectation. In order to determine whether such a dynamic might indeed be the result of a self-fulfilling prophecy, the researchers first tested for differences between the interaction styles of White subjects interviewing Black candidates and those interviewing Whites. In a second study, they compared the interview performances of a different group of White subjects, some of whom were treated similarly to the Black candidates and others of whom were treated similarly to the White candidates from the first study.

Earlier studies had found that individuals tend to avoid and cut short interaction with "stigmatized" persons, such as those with a physical disability, and that individuals' attitudes toward another person are reflected in their nonverbal behavior toward that person. More positive attitudes toward a target person result in an individual's maintaining more "immediate" behaviors—including "closer interpersonal distances, more eye contact, more direct shoulder orientation, and more forward lean."[41] In the first interview experiment, Word and his colleagues used these and related behaviors as measures of the degree of "immediacy" that White interviewers employed in interacting with White and Black interviewees. All the interviewees had been trained beforehand to act in a standardized way both as to the content of their answers and their nonverbal behavior, and they were monitored to ensure that they maintained standard behaviors throughout the interviews. As each White interviewer-subject interviewed a White and then a Black applicant (or vice versa), two judges scored the interviewers' immediacy behaviors.

Overall, the Black applicants received less immediate behaviors from White interviewers than did White applicants. Specifically, the interviewers physically placed themselves farther away from the Black applicants, interviewed them for shorter periods of time, and committed a higher rate of speech errors (such as sentence changes, repetitions, stuttering, incomplete sentences, and "intruding, incoherent sounds") with Black than with White applicants. From these results, the researchers concluded that Black applicants were treated with less immediacy than White applicants, consistent with Blackness being viewed as a stigmatizing trait.

In the second experiment, the researchers examined the effect on a job applicant's performance of being treated with less immediate behaviors. They removed the applicant's race as a factor in performance by using only White subjects in this experiment. Because this time they were interested in examining the interview*ees*' behavior in response to being treated with or without immediacy, the researchers trained two interviewers to act differently with respect to the factors on which the interviewers in the first experiment had shown significant differences (speech error rate, length of interview, and physical distance from applicant): one behaved precisely as the interviewers had behaved toward White applicants (the "immediate" condition), and one behaved precisely as the interviewers had behaved toward Black applicants (the "nonimmediate" condition). On all other behaviors they were trained to act similarly. Then, interviews with subjects in the two conditions were rated by both nonparticipant judges and the subjects themselves.

The results confirmed the operation of a self-fulfilling prophecy: the applicants who were treated more negatively were judged both to perform more poorly than the other applicants and to respond to the interviewers with less favorable behaviors of their own. The judges rated the applicants in the nonimmediate condition as performing less adequately and being less calm and composed than applicants in the immediate condition. In addition, applicants in the nonimmediate condition reciprocated the interviewer's negative nonverbal behaviors by moving their chairs farther away from the interviewer's when given the opportunity to move through a contrived interruption in the interview. In contrast, applicants in the immediate condition moved their chairs closer to the interviewer's, committed fewer speech errors, and generally responded with more immediate behaviors, such as forward lean, eye contact, and direct shoulder orientation. Finally, applicants in the nonimmediate condition rated their interviewers as less friendly and less adequate overall than did applicants in the immediate condition.

Word and his colleagues pointed out the important implications of this two-stage experiment: "The present results suggest that analyses of black-and-white interactions, particularly in the area of job-seeking Blacks in white society, might profit if it were assumed that the 'problem' of black performance resides not entirely within the Blacks, but rather within the interaction setting itself."[42]

Subsequent studies have reproduced this behavioral confirmation process, further documenting the situation-defining and self-fulfilling nature of social stereotypes associated with race and gender.[43] Recent experiments have even shown that behavioral confirmation of stereotypes can occur when the stereotype is not consciously activated—for example, when a stereotype is cued subliminally by a stimulus outside the perceiver's awareness.[44]

Behavioral Confirmation of Stereotypes in Real Life

Collectively, these studies suggest that the behavioral confirmation process can have a significant effect on social interactions when racial and other group-based stereotypes come into play. Specifically, they show that stereotypes can define the terms of an interaction by inducing the perceiver to treat the target in a way that "boxes in" the target by giving him or her little choice but to act according to, and therefore in confirmation of, the stereotype. In other words, the perceiver's expectations become a feature of the situation that act to "channel" the interaction so as to create their own confirming evidence. Stereotypes therefore can be perpetuated and even strengthened *despite* their inaccuracy.

Nevertheless, and although it has consistently been produced in the laboratory and confirmed empirically, some might point out that the behavioral confirmation of expectations is not inevitable.[45] Sometimes people are surprised by others who act inconsistently with their expectations, and perceivers may themselves seek out disconfirming information. Even in laboratory settings, behavioral confirmation of expectations does not occur in every perceiver-target interaction, and a few experiments have even produced evidence of self-disconfirming (or "suicidal") prophecies.[46]

Outside the laboratory we may expect behavioral confirmation to be even less consistent. For one thing, real-life interactions often bear little resemblance to the neatly arranged, highly artificial encounters produced in an experimental setting. In daily life, people's expectations about others are not usually supplied or triggered by an outside party's manipulations, nor do people's dealings proceed in as isolated or orderly a fashion as in researcher-contrived interactions. In addition, individuals are not relegated to simple roles as either "perceiver" or "target"; in authentic interactions, both participants play both roles, and so each person's expectations of the other will come into play. Further, in day-to-day interactions the participants may be motivated by various goals that influence the way they deal with one another. For example, someone who is motivated to make an accurate judgment about another person—perhaps because he depends on her to work with him on a project, knows that he will later be required to justify his assessment, or simply has been asked to form an accurate impression—may consciously refrain from imposing his expectations on the other person, may be more attentive to the effect of the situation on (as well as disconfirming evidence in) her behavior, and may seek more individuating information about her. Whichever of these behaviors the person adopts gives the other person the opportunity to act inconsistently with the perceiver's expectations. Similarly, someone who is motivated to get another person to like him will behave in a more open (even an ingratiating) way that is less likely to produce a self-fulfilling outcome.[47]

Even the random particulars of the situation—such as whether or not the parties are in a hurry, whether they are focused on one another or distracted by some other concerns—may affect whether their interaction follows the textbook pattern. Moreover, although the behavioral confirmation model stresses the power of the perceiver in defining the situation and limiting the target's options in terms of how to respond, we should not underestimate the desire, and sometimes even the power, of an individual in the target position to "disconfirm" the perceiver's expectations. Someone who becomes aware of another's negative impression of her and feels threatened by that view may choose to behave in ways that visibly disconfirm expectations. I could have held my ground with the doctor and remained dry-eyed; I am quite sure that eventually he would have let me leave.

These means for disrupting the process are supported in the literature and suggest that human interaction is not hopelessly mired in a vicious circle of self-fulfilling prophecy. Nevertheless, behavioral confirmation of negative expectations is highly reliable in the types of interactions that may have the most far-reaching effects on some groups' vulnerability to discrimination and access to opportunity, as well as on the perpetuation and entrenchment of the negative stereotypes that influence both. Interactions in a range of settings in which group-based discrimination is a perpetual concern—such as employment, health care, and the criminal justice system—tend to be characterized by the presence of factors that promote behavioral confirmation and the absence of factors that might disrupt the process. In these settings, the types of expectations at issue, the typical power differences between the parties, the parties' respective roles in and goals for their interaction, the circumstances under which they interact, and the institutional practices that structure their encounter all come together to limit the target's options for acting other than in confirmation of negative stereotypes.

First, while some expectations of the kind tested in laboratory settings (for example, that a random target is hostile or extroverted) might be harder to create and more easily dashed, negative cultural and social stereotypes are the very kind of expectations that have the strongest influence on interactions and the greatest likelihood of being behaviorally confirmed. They tend to be held with more certainty than other interpersonal expectancies because they are shared and validated by others—often by society at large. In addition, group-based stereotypes are often both automatically activated and chronically accessible, and therefore are insidious and powerful in coloring perceivers' interpretations of interactions.

Even when perceivers are aware of the influence of those stereotypes and try to resist acting on them, they might have difficulty doing so—or might even aggravate the stereotypes' influence. That is, the fear of appearing racist might introduce a kind of stereotype threat into the situation that causes a person to "choke" in an interracial encounter, and then to behave in a way that is more prejudiced than he feels.[48] On the other hand, trying not to be seen as prejudiced might also help to *prevent* behavioral confirmation by leading a person to behave more agreeably toward his partner. Behaving more agreeably has the dual advantages, as we have seen, of enabling a person to form a more accurate impression of his partner and of making the interaction more pleasant for that person. Because of the stress associated with trying to be seen as egalitarian, however, the perceiver who is working to overcome his biases might enjoy the interaction less and therefore like the target less.[49]

Further, negative stereotypes of minority groups tend to come into play within interactions that are structured to favor their behavioral confirmation, because "the same people who are typically the targets of social and cultural stereotypes are often those who have less power in our society (e.g., members of minority groups)."[50] The mere existence of a power differential plays a significant role in behavioral confirmation because it structures the real-life interaction similarly to a laboratory setup, in which one party clearly functions as perceiver and the other as target. While both parties literally bring their own expectations of one another into their interaction, the more powerful of the two tends to set the tone for the interaction, thereby functioning as the perceiver. Further, in the settings that raise the most concern, the roles of perceiver and target are designated consistently with the power differential: the interviewer evaluates the interviewee's suitability for employment; the doctor diagnoses and formulates treatment options for the patient; and the police officer assesses the suspect's likely guilt or innocence.

In addition to structuring the interaction in a way that promotes textbook behavioral confirmation, the power differential influences the parties' goals for the encounter, and therefore each party's choice of an interaction strategy. The perceiver's goals play an important part in determining whether she gives the target opportunities to disconfirm expectations or instead boxes the target in to behaving so as to confirm her expectations. For example, a perceiver who seeks to intimidate the target or to establish her superior position might treat the target in an unfriendly or contemptuous manner, thereby constraining the target's options for responding and setting off a confirmatory chain of events. Further, the more powerful perceiver may not be aware of her biased expectations, may not be motivated to form an accurate impression of the target, or may even be motivated to confirm her preformed judgment of the target.

These motivations can promote behavioral confirmation even in situations in which the perceiver's goal is to learn about the target for purposes of making a decision about him, for the goal of acquiring knowledge is not necessarily the same as the goal of making an accurate assessment, which tends to allow for disconfirmation of expectations. Some settings—for example, interviewing or counseling situations or teacher-student relationships—might activate a perceiver's desire to get a stable and predictable view of the target, as opposed to an accurate one, so she can perform her duties of assessment:

> [T]herapists and counselors need to know what to expect from their clients, typically having to make assessments of their clients' well-being and their prognosis for improvement in treatment. Employers also seek a predictable view of job candidates, oftentimes trying to decide during the job interview what they are like and how they will perform on the job. Similarly, teachers often are tempted to make quick judgments of their students and get

> an idea of what kind of learning curves they can expect from them.[51]

Sometimes, too, people just want to believe that the world is stable and predictable and that they can rely on their "beliefs, expectations, preconceptions, hunches, and stereotypes" to guide their interactions with other people.[52]

In such cases, the powerful perceiver tends to find her expectations confirmed, and it is not hard to see why: a person in this position will tend to limit the amount of information that she gathers and therefore needs to process (perhaps by asking the target biased and leading rather than open-ended questions), to focus on information that is consistent with her expectations, to interpret ambiguous information as confirming those expectations, and to elicit expectation-confirming behavior from the target. Moreover, even if the target's behavior is ambiguous, the perceiver (and third parties) may view it as consistent with expectations due to the general tendency of observers to interpret the ambiguous behavior of another person in accordance with the observer's expectations, and the specific tendency to interpret ambiguous behavior in conformity with racial stereotypes.

In turn, a lower status, less powerful target realistically has fewer options in choosing an interaction strategy. Assuming he is aware of the perceiver's expectations, a target sometimes can disconfirm expectations by failing or refusing to accommodate the perceiver's definition of the situation. However, a target who is subordinate to the perceiver is not likely to even try to do so, especially if he determines that it is not in his self-interest to respond inconsistently with the perceiver's overtures. A target may have a number of reasons for choosing to defer to the perceiver's script. Sometimes a target simply feels that it is not worth making the effort to challenge the perceiver's views because the consequences of being misperceived are trivial. It didn't really matter to me, for example, whether or not the doctor thought I was a typical emotional female—I just wanted to get out of his office.

In many situations involving a more powerful perceiver, on the other hand, the target may feel that he has little choice but to defer, because he has too much to lose by challenging the perceiver's script. Social norms generally discourage disconfirming behavior, and a target sometimes pays a heavy social price for violating the rules. Especially if the target depends on the perceiver's goodwill in order to avoid a negative outcome, the wiser course may be simply to take "the line of least resistance" by responding in accordance with her overtures, even if it results in confirming her expectations about him.[53] A lower-status target also may see an advantage to behaving in conformity with the perceiver's expectations, because he or she may anticipate being rewarded for so complying. For example, a woman interviewing for a job with an employer who holds traditional views of women's appropriate roles and behavior might dress and act in a more stereotypically feminine way in order to increase her chances of being hired.[54] In some cases, the target in such a situation may not be able to avoid being perceived consistently with the stereotype no matter how he behaves, because his actions may be interpreted in a biased fashion by the other anyway.

Other aspects of the situation may reinforce these tendencies or add new pressures toward behavioral confirmation. Sometimes the situation simply does not present the opportunity for disconfirming behavior, because it is not the type of setting in which the target has a chance to act in ways that challenge the perceiver's expectations. If the parties interact in a situation where set procedures must be followed, such as a classroom or a medical office, the target may have a limited range of choices in terms of how to respond. Some qualities that the perceiver attributes to the target—attitudes or beliefs, for example—might be internal traits that are not easily disconfirmed through behavior. And sometimes the parties simply lack the cognitive or behavioral resources to do more than resort by default to stereotype-confirming patterns of behavior and interpretation. For example, the perceiver may be under too much stress or too busy to do much more than rely on cognitive and behavioral shortcuts. People who are physiologically or emotionally aroused or under greater cognitive load may rely more heavily on expectations and stereotypes.[55] One study even found that "*morning people* (i.e., those who reach their peak of cognitive functioning early in the day) are more likely to rely on their stereotypes at night," while the opposite was the case with "night people."[56] Time pressures also limit the ability and motivation of both parties to avoid stereotype confirmation. Under these constraints, perceivers will find it easier to both see and treat the target consistently with expectations, and the target likewise may find it easier to get through the interaction by complying with the perceiver's script for their interaction.

Behavioral Confirmation in Context: Self-Fulfilling Stereotypes of Criminality

As we have seen, a wide range of expectations and stereotypes can sometimes produce their own confirmation, even when those expectations are wholly without foundation. The consequences of behavioral confirmation also can vary, depending on the content of the stereotype and the situation in which it comes into play. It may matter little, for example, whether a new acquaintance at a party develops an erroneous impression of you if you are unlikely to see that person again. With some stereotypes, on the other hand, the consequences can be dire and even life threatening.

An especially powerful stereotype with far-reaching effects links the members of some social groups with expectations of criminality and deviance. It is well known that men of color—whether Black, Latino, Middle Eastern, or Asian—are often seen as violent, aggressive, or treacherous. Gay men also are stereotyped as deviant or criminal; they may be viewed, for example, as sexually promiscuous or predatory.[57] Aside from its obvious influence in the criminal justice process itself (an example of which will be explored below), this kind of association has implications for the way members of those groups are treated and respond in a variety of settings as mundane as retail transactions and as serious as health care. Later we will explore one example, seeing how the expectation that a Black male patient will be aggressive or violent can cause doctors to treat him in a racially prejudiced manner, leading the patient to act in conformity with the stereotype and the clinician to make a more severe diagnosis or to recommend a more restrictive intervention than might actually be warranted—but which appears to be completely justified.

Stereotypes of criminality can infiltrate ordinary daily transactions as well. For example, some individuals routinely encounter a private form of racial profiling ("shopping while Black" or Brown) in which they are watched, followed, questioned, and even accosted by store managers, salespeople, and security guards who have absorbed the stereotype that people of color are likely to shoplift. Many of these shoppers are well aware of these suspicions. Some may try to head off trouble by playing against the stereotype, to "prov[e] themselves to be worthy shoppers"[58]—dressing in their finest clothes, using sophisticated language and mannerisms, buying things they don't really want, or tipping extra generously for even substandard service. But their awareness of store personnel's mistrust and scrutiny also can lead shoppers to behave in ways that appear to confirm that they can't be trusted or to justify harsh or aggressive treatment. An individual may act nervous or paranoid out of concern that she will be mistaken for a shoplifter, or she may confront store personnel whom she perceives to be treating her with suspicion or disrespect. This behavior, in turn, can itself become an objective basis for stopping and questioning the shopper, for denying her service or excluding her from the premises, or even for physically restraining the shopper or calling the police.[59]

In a similar way, everyday encounters with police can turn confrontational based on little more than each side's expectation of trouble. These expectations are confirmed when the following sequence plays out:

> (1) police approach black citizens with undue suspicion; (2) blacks often anticipate unfair treatment from officers and thus withhold

> respect and deference, which is conducive to harsh police reactions; and (3) the very exercise of police authority (often brusque and authoritarian) may be mistakenly construed by citizens as symptomatic of racial discrimination, again leading to conflicts that result in punitive treatment of black citizens.[60]

Stereotypes of criminality also come into play at various points later in the criminal justice process. Volumes have been written on the influence of racial stereotypes in law enforcement, on prosecutorial decision making, at trial, and in sentencing. One particular transaction in the criminal justice process—police interrogations of criminal suspects—provides an almost textbook example of the potential for behavioral confirmation of erroneous expectations and a vivid illustration of the real-life consequences of this dynamic.[61] The outcome of an interrogation can determine whether a person goes free or is prosecuted, and ultimately may influence whether he is acquitted or convicted and the severity of his sentence.

There is good reason to believe, and initial experimental evidence to support the belief, that these interactions have great potential to produce behavioral confirmation of erroneous expectations of guilt. An interrogation that does elicit false confirmation of guilt—particularly one that results in a false *confession*—has serious consequences for the suspect. Not only does the encounter fail to bring an end to the criminal investigation, but the suspect's behavior tends to be viewed as especially persuasive evidence of his guilt.[62] Furthermore, the behavioral confirmation of erroneous expectations of guilt would compound, and certainly would not check, the effect of racial bias in the criminal justice system to the extent that race already acts as a proxy for criminality in decisions that are made at various points throughout the criminal justice process.

The intent to obtain a false confession is not necessary for behavioral confirmation to occur, or even a false confession to be elicited, if the interrogator believes the suspect is guilty. Whether or not the interrogator intends to produce false evidence of guilt, the interrogation is structured almost ideally to allow for such a result.

First, the interrogator enters the interaction with a strong expectation—"predisposed and reasonably certain of the suspect's guilt"[63]—because standard practice is to interrogate only those suspects whom investigators have determined are likely to be guilty based on a preliminary interview. As two experts on false confessions have stated:

> Although there is little evidence that American police intend to extract confessions from the innocent, they too frequently become so zealously committed to a preconceived belief in a suspect's guilt or so reliant on their interrogation methods that they mistakenly extract an uncorroborated, inconsistent, and manifestly untrue confession. Too often interrogators appear to give no thought to the possibility that the confession they have extracted could be false.[64]

The strength with which this belief is held may not be warranted, however. The determination of guilt often is based on an officer's assessment that the suspect is lying when he denies the allegations against him, and it may not be supported by external evidence. Moreover, studies have shown that "even experienced detectives" may not achieve better than "chance-level" accuracy in distinguishing between true and false denials of guilt, although they may be quite confident in their judgments.[65]

Second, the interrogation of a criminal suspect may be the epitome of the goal-driven social interaction. While the interrogator's explicit purpose may be to get a truthful statement, if she believes the suspect is guilty the interrogator will define a successful interrogation as one that results in a confession. Interrogators may use a number of strategies to achieve that goal and, by definition, to deny the suspect the opportunity to disconfirm the expectation of guilt. The interrogator uses this goal to set the tone of the interaction, as the standard interrogation manual advises interrogators to "convince the suspect that he has no doubt as to the suspect's guilt."[66] Techniques designed to prod the suspect toward confessing include suggesting that forensic evidence of his guilt exists when in fact none has been found, or pretending to sympathize with the suspect, perhaps by minimizing the "moral seriousness" of the offense or suggesting a more palatable motivation for the crime than the one that is presumed. Interrogators are advised to "communicate[] to the suspect the futility of maintaining his innocence"[67] and to resist the suspect's attempts to deny his guilt. Interrogators may, in fact, become so fixated on obtaining a confession that they ignore disconfirming evidence that the suspect offers.

Moreover, the social structure of the interrogation is ideal for producing behavioral confirmation of the interrogator's expectations, because she is both the perceiver and the more powerful of the two parties. Not only does her role require her to question and evaluate the suspect, but she also has the ability to control both the course of the interrogation itself and the fate of the suspect, and she may play up those abilities whenever it seems strategically expedient to do so. The standard interrogation manual suggests, for example, that the interrogator conduct the interrogation in private, "emphasize his complete control of the situation [by] requir[ing] the suspect to wait alone in the interrogation room for a brief period before meeting with him," and "invade the suspect's body space, direct him to be seated if he attempts to stand, and prohibit him from smoking or fidgeting."[68] The interrogator also may manipulate the suspect by leading him to believe that she will act to procure a benefit for him if he confesses.[69]

The suspect, on the other hand, may tend to be deferential and accommodating, *especially* if he is innocent and believes that he should continue responding to questions in order to clear up the interrogator's mistaken belief that he is guilty. However, because she has been trained to ignore the suspect's protestations, to maintain her attitude of certainty, and to systematically break down the suspect's resistance, the interrogator is not likely to relent in pursuing a confession. Instead, she is likely to continue to try to convince the overborne suspect that it is in his best interest to confess.

Experts have explained that even an innocent suspect may end up believing that he is better off confessing if the interrogator is successful at creating the impression that he has little chance of "surviving police questioning without being arrested and punished."[70] Both guilty and innocent suspects may come to view confessing as a rational choice because interrogators are trained to manipulate a suspect's perception of his situation, convincing him "either that he has been caught (if he is guilty) or that his situation is hopeless (if he is innocent), that further denial is pointless and that it is in his self-interest to confess."[71] Even if the suspect continues to maintain his innocence, moreover, the interrogator may continue to believe he is guilty, because she may interpret his denials as being deceptive or defensive. However, as one writer has pointed out, although interrogators may believe that they can distinguish between truthful and deceptive suspects, few people—including law enforcement officers—are able to do so. In fact, some supposed indications of deception are equally consistent with the anxiety that an innocent suspect would display because he is "overwhelmed by the dynamics of the interrogation process."[72]

A recent experimental study by Saul M. Kassin and his colleagues found that when interrogators employed standard practices, the potential for confirmation of erroneous expectations of guilt was high.[73] Regardless of the guilt or innocence of the suspects they questioned, interrogators who entered the interrogation believing that most suspects were guilty chose to ask more guilt-presumptive questions, used more interrogation techniques, and more frequently perceived suspects as being guilty than did interrogators who believed that most suspects were innocent. Regardless of their actual guilt or innocence, moreover, suspects who were expected to be guilty behaved consistently with expectations, for they became "noticeably more defensive."

Further—and, as the researchers noted, "paradoxical[ly]" and "disturbing[ly]"—interrogators with an expectation of guilt exerted the most pressure to confess on suspects who were actually innocent and therefore provided plausible accounts of their activities during the relevant time period. Indeed, the *innocent* suspects

> [b]rought out the worst in the guilt-presumptive interrogators. . . . Interrogators who approached the task with a guilty base-rate expectation never stopped to reevaluate this belief—even when paired with innocent suspects who issued plausible denials. Rather, it appears that they interpreted the denials as proof of a guilty person's resistance—and redoubled their efforts to elicit a confession.[74]

Finally, neither interrogators nor third-party observers were able to distinguish between truthful (innocent) and deceptive (guilty) suspects: "In short, a presumption of guilt triggered aggressive interrogations, which constrained the behavior of suspects and led others to infer their guilt—thus confirming the initial presumption"[75]—regardless of whether or not that presumption was correct.

The researchers pointed out that the *observers'* inability to determine that an innocent suspect was telling the truth has the "most devastating" implications. First, the observers *were* able to distinguish between interrogators with guilty and innocent expectations, and perceived the former as putting more pressure on suspects and working harder to get a confession. Second, observers considered the innocent suspects' denials to be more plausible than those of the guilty suspects. Nevertheless, observers *still* were more likely to consider a suspect's behavior defensive and judge him to be guilty if the interrogator expected him to be guilty. In other words, despite being aware of the situational constraints under which the suspects labored, observers failed to consider how those constraints might have influenced the suspects' behavior and ultimately judged them in accordance with the presumptions of the interrogator. The observers thus "committed the fundamental attribution error," by failing to correct the impressions they drew from the suspect's behavior to account for the chain of events set in motion by the interrogator's initial presumption of guilt.

Nor are existing legal controls likely to account for the behavioral confirmation process through which erroneous expectations can contribute to determinations of guilt. The standard psychological interrogation techniques described above are not, generally speaking, unlawful, so law enforcement agencies have no incentive not to employ them and are unlikely to face sanctions (such as the inadmissibility of the statement obtained) if they do.[76] Guilt-consistent responses of suspects in such interrogations—perhaps even including false confessions—are likely to be taken by law enforcement officers at face value, and therefore will promote the decision to prosecute and perhaps be used to press the suspect for a guilty plea. As Kassin's study shows, moreover, the suspect's behavior may be read as consistent with guilt even if it is ambiguous or includes plausible denials of guilt. If the case goes to trial and the defendant's statement is admitted into evidence, Kassin's study suggests that jurors are unlikely to factor into their assessments of guilt the extent to which the suspect's apparently guilty behavior might have been influenced by the conditions of the interrogation. This may be the case even if the court instructs the jury to consider the conditions of the interrogation in evaluating the defendant's statement, because jurors may be unable to disregard a statement once they have heard it.[77]

For suspects of all colors, the potential for the behavioral confirmation of erroneous expectations of guilt is real. To the extent that a suspect's race contributes to the interrogator's belief in his guilt, however, the danger is even greater. Furthermore, the mock juror study discussed in chapter 2 suggests that jurors may be even less willing or able to discount inculpatory but potentially faulty evidence when the suspect is not White.[78] Compounding these effects is the possibility that the judge who instructs the jury herself will be influenced by racial stereotypes, believe the defendant to be guilty, and unconsciously transmit that belief to the jurors.[79] The "danger[] of presuming guilt,"[80] then—especially for suspects of color—is that, even in the absence of individual actors' intent to convict an innocent person, an erroneous expectation of guilt sometimes both creates its own confirmation and conceals its effect in producing that confirmation, leaving only objective "evidence" on which to base final judgment.

4

Failures of Imagination

When Pat Tillman walked away from a $3.6 million contract and a promising career in the National Football League to join the Army Rangers, his decision astounded football fans and nonfans alike. When Tillman was killed in the line of duty in Afghanistan, his death evoked an outpouring of tributes from political leaders, sports figures, and ordinary people and, some suggested, overshadowed the deaths of soldiers from more ordinary backgrounds who also had perished in Afghanistan or Iraq. When the military later announced that Tillman had probably been killed by "friendly fire"—that he was mistakenly shot by members of his own platoon—the announcement made his death seem all the more tragic.[1]

Few people would be likely to suggest that Tillman's death was, in fact, more tragic than the deaths of those other soldiers. If it was not, then why did his death draw so much more notice and trigger so much stronger a reaction than the death of any other individual soldier in Afghanistan or Iraq? One obvious reason is that Tillman did not match our expectations of who becomes a soldier; the life he walked away from was not one we can imagine most people giving up to join the military. He was an unlikely soldier, and his death in the line of duty seemed more poignant because of that.

To learn further that Tillman died from friendly rather than enemy fire only heightened that feeling. Although deaths from friendly fire are not uncommon during war, they evoke stronger reactions than deaths from enemy fire. People feel worse about a death from friendly fire and view it as a greater hardship for the soldier's family than one from enemy fire. The greater poignancy of deaths from friendly fire cannot be attributed to differences in the severity of the survivors' losses, however. Nor can it be due to a sense that the victim of friendly fire has higher moral standing than a victim of enemy fire. Rather, what makes it more devastating is the sense that a death from friendly fire should not have occurred, because it is incongruous with our expectations of war: soldiers' deaths during war are not "supposed" to come at the hands of their comrades. Because those deaths are not supposed to happen, the victims are viewed as more innocent than those who die in a more congruous fashion, and their deaths strike us as more unjust.[2]

As Tillman's story shows, a sense of incongruity can arise on account of *how* something happens, and it can be evoked by *who* it is that suffers a particular misfortune. Consequently, our sympathy and concern often vary according to how normal or abnormal we perceive someone's plight to be. As Richard Delgado has pointed out, this tendency has disturbing implications:

> If you see an upper-class white family being evicted from their nice suburban home, you feel alarmed because you know that sort of situation is abnormal for them. You realize they must be experiencing real distress. But if you see starving Biafrans on TV, you feel less empathy because you know that is their ordinary situation. Famines are common in that part of the world, so your heart does not go out to them as it would to a neighbor who materialized on your doorstep not having eaten in eight days.[3]

Delgado suggests that this bias may also account for the differences in people's willingness to help Black and White persons in distress that we saw in chapter 2. People may be less apt to help a Black person not because of simple racism, but because the Black person's hardship seems normal: "Everyone assumes the black person has a rough road in life."[4]

A social-psychological approach called norm theory explains these differential levels of empathy. Norm theory holds that people's reactions to events depend on the degree to which the events depart from their view of what is normal or to be expected.[5] Put very plainly, "People do not like that which is abnormal."[6] But, as leading norm theorists Daniel Kahneman and Dale T. Miller have explained, "The correlation between the perception of abnormality of an event and the intensity of the affective reaction to it . . . can have consequences that violate other rules of justice."[7] Delgado's examples show, for example, that our preference for what is normal predisposes us to sympathize more with those who typically suffer less and inures us to the pain of those whose hardships we expect. In addition to accounting for our biased affective reactions to negative events, norm theory reveals our tendency to develop biased explanations for why bad things happen to people, as well as to place blame and dispense sympathy accordingly. Norm theory also illuminates yet another way in which stereotypes are constructed and reinforced by showing that the normality bias works not just in hindsight, but also has enduring, prospective effects. Norm theory illuminates, in other words, how our responses to discrimination both lead us to accept discriminatory outcomes *by* default and reinforce the designation of those outcomes *as* the default.

In order to understand why our bias toward normality has these far-reaching consequences, we must first understand the psychological mechanism by which it comes into play when we think about an event after it has occurred.

Counterfactual Thinking and the Normality Bias

People react to events by thinking about not just what happened, but also what did *not* happen. After missing the bus to work, for example, a person might think, "If only I had not stopped to buy a newspaper, I would have caught the bus." When their team loses a close game in the final seconds, disappointed basketball fans may think ruefully about how different the result would have been if their team had successfully converted more foul shots earlier in the game. This phenomenon is known as counterfactual thinking: thinking about what might have been instead of what was, or thinking that is "literally, contrary to the facts."[8] Counterfactual thinking often occurs spontaneously, but it also can arise in response to a question or prompt. Legal judgments frequently call for counterfactual thinking. "But for" causation, for example, asks a fact finder to engage in counterfactual thinking to determine whether or not particular acts or omissions contributed to an outcome.[9] Historians sometimes engage in counterfactual thinking too, as a way of assessing the importance or influence of various factors in producing pivotal events. A historian might ask, for example, "What if Frank Wills, the night watchman at the Watergate office building in Washington, D.C., had not noticed on the night of June 17, 1972 that the basement garage doors had been taped open? Would Watergate still be 'just an upscale address'?"[10]

Counterfactual thinking influences our emotional reactions to an event. A person may feel happy or sad based on a comparison between what happened and what almost or might have happened. A driver who just misses colliding with another vehicle feels fortunate because he can so easily imagine the avoided accident happening, while someone who holds a lottery ticket that is one digit off the winning number feels sad and unlucky because she could so easily have won the jackpot.[11] People's counterfactual-based reactions may not match their objective circumstances. Studies of Olympic medalists and other elite athletes found that silver medalists were less happy than bronze medalists because of the contrasting content of their counterfactual thoughts: silver medalists thought about how close they came to winning the gold, while bronze medalists were pleased to have won a medal at all, thinking that they could easily have placed fourth instead.[12]

The direction—and, as Pat Tillman's story shows, the intensity—of our reactions to events depend on the content of the counterfactuals to which we compare them. Norm theory explains that their content depends, in turn, on the ease with which we construct those counterfactual alternatives—that is, the event's "mutability."[13] The event's mutability may explain the intensity of his supporters' reactions to Senator John F. Kerry's loss in the 2004 presidential election. With exit polls early on Election Day showing Kerry leading incumbent President George W. Bush—in some states by wide margins—Kerry supporters could easily imagine Kerry winning and were especially devastated by his defeat.[14]

Our counterfactual thoughts are biased toward normality because we have difficulty imagining alternatives to scenarios that we perceive as normal, routine, or unexceptional, but can easily recast events that strike us as surprising or unusual. The latter can be altered simply by mentally shifting the exceptional to a more normal state, because that counterfactual world comes easily to mind. As a result, people react strongly to exceptional events because they compare them to what they view as normal, but will readily accept an expected or taken-for-granted state of affairs that does not elicit counterfactual thoughts. And while an event's normality is the chief determinant of its mutability, other factors also can affect the ease and likelihood of constructing counterfactual alternatives. Mutable events tend to be characterized by some sense of "deviance."[15] For example, just as an unusual event is more mutable than a routine one, a person's action is easier to undo than her inaction, and behaviors that are controllable are more readily imagined differently than those that are uncontrollable.[16]

Differences in the mental mutability or perceived normality of events can have far-reaching consequences, because a chain of assessments follows our initial affective reactions. When something bad happens, whether to ourselves or someone else, we want to understand why. We engage in counterfactual thinking in order to explain why the event happened, and the more mutable (less normal) features of an event tend to take on greater causal significance. How easily we can mutate the behavior of the people concerned also influences our explanations for the event, our evaluations of the parties, and our assessments of blame and sympathy. Furthermore, our affective reactions tend to reinforce or amplify those assessments, so that we feel greater sympathy for or attribute less blame to a person the more we identify or empathize with him and, conversely, view less sympathetically or judge more harshly a person toward whom we have a less favorable reaction.[17] Generally speaking, then, the more abnormal or mutable a fact or event is, the more salient it will be, the more intense the reaction it will elicit, the more likely it is to be identified as causal, and the stronger the evaluations that will result. Finally, we use the products of counterfactual thinking—whether they be legal or social judgments—to assess conduct and conditions, and thereby to set standards. Consequently, counterfactual thinking does not just draw on but also defines and constructs norms.[18]

But the mutability of a fact or an event hardly seems a compelling basis on which to make a judgment, for mutability often does not align with justice or reason. The various factors that affect mutability may, but need not, coincide with objective grounds for condemnation or compensation, such as the probability, foreseeability, severity, or fairness of an outcome.[19] What we consider to be normal, for example, corresponds with what we expect or have grown accustomed to, so the normality of an event simply describes our inability to imagine an alternative to it,[20] and judgments made by reference to what is normal are in that respect merely judgments by default. As is by now commonplace to point out, moreover, what we expect or are used to may simply reflect biased and unjust social models. Social group stereotypes are "normal"—they come easily and often unbidden to mind and are difficult to shake—but they tend to be neither accurate as a descriptive matter nor egalitarian in their prescriptions. Similarly, social scripts and schemas for how things are "supposed" to happen may merely reflect a tradition of discriminatory practices.[21]

Other factors that determine mutability also may form a faulty basis for reasoning and judgment because they are often random or arbitrary. In one set of experiments, mock jurors recommended greater punishment for a burglar and felt greater sympathy for his victims when the burglary occurred the night before the victims returned from a three-month vacation than when it occurred in the middle of the three-month period. Although the degree of wrongdoing and size of the material losses were the same in both situations, the timing of the burglary made a difference in terms of how easily jurors could mutate it by imagining it not happening.[22]

Because the mere perception of mutability may be sufficient to bias our reactions and evaluations, erroneous assumptions about the characteristics of a person or the features of a situation may lead to faulty judgments as well. For example, we may accept racism as normal because we assume that bigots are driven by irrational tastes and prejudices, without realizing that in some situations racist behavior is calculated and well within a person's control.[23] Some recent studies have suggested, moreover, that counterfactual thinking is not purely objective and data-driven, but may be influenced by existing attitudes and beliefs. That is, in generating counterfactual thoughts following an event, people sometimes are motivated to mutate that antecedent event that supports reasoning that is consistent with their existing beliefs. As a result, they tend to interpret the event in a way that reinforces, rather than challenges, their existing beliefs and biases.[24] Finally, the judgments that result from counterfactual thinking can be *applied* in a biased fashion: in one study that examined how counterfactual thinking operates alongside normative ambiguity, subjects who reviewed narratives of the same accident in which only the race of the driver was changed blamed the Black driver more than the White counterpart for causing the accident by engaging in the same mutable conduct. Notice that the subjects showed no racial bias in assessing the *mutability* of the drivers' behavior, but they did *judge* the Black driver more severely than the White driver based on their equally mutable actions—probably because, in a normatively ambiguous situation that supplied a legitimate basis for assessing a harsh judgment, they could attribute those judgments to a nonracial factor.[25]

As we shall see, if left unchecked, biases in our counterfactual analysis can lead us to enact a "counterfactual fallacy": to confuse "what *might have been* the case and what *ought to have been* the case."[26] More to the point, we may confuse what *normally* is the case with what *should* be the case.

The Normalcy and Normalization of Discrimination

Because counterfactual thinking influences our reactions to and explanations of negative events, biases in counterfactual thinking have the potential to distort our assessments of discriminatory outcomes at several levels. First, they can mute our reactions to discrimination generally, leading us to tolerate and even to accept unequal outcomes. Our acceptance of discrimination is not due solely to a general indifference or hardness toward groups that are vulnerable to discrimination, but results in part from the specific ways in which our preference for the normal or customary affects how we process and evaluate events and behavior. That is, the normality bias leads us to react less strongly to (and perhaps to not even notice) misfortunes that we take for granted or that follow an expected pattern. This bias also promotes the entrenchment of those patterns because it leads us to accept the established order but to find jarring, and therefore to resist, challenges to those accepted ways. Furthermore, it makes it easier for us to justify the established patterns by viewing them as rational and even fair.

Second, when a case of alleged discrimination does come under scrutiny, biases in counterfactual thinking can distort our causal explanations of the events in question and our evaluations of the parties. Because determining whether discrimination has occurred is "fundamentally an exercise in causal attribution,"[27] the relative normality or mutability of the parties' conduct can influence our judgments of their roles in producing the outcome in a way that leads us to reduce the perpetrator's responsibility and ascribe undue responsibility to the victim. More broadly, our judgments of blame and sympathy create a feedback loop that reinforces the norms, expectations, and practices that contributed to our biased judgments and perpetuate discriminatory reactions and behavior.

Immutable Wrongs and Suitable Victims

The more easily we can imagine the victim of a tragic fate avoiding it, the more badly we will feel that he has suffered, so that the level of sympathy we feel and the amount of compensation we dole out may turn on trivial differences in the circumstances of a tragedy. In the burglary study discussed earlier, for example, subjects expressed greater sympathy for victims if their homes were burglarized the night before they returned from vacation than if the burglary occurred several weeks before their return. Similarly, subjects in another study recommended significantly higher compensatory awards for a convenience store customer who was shot during a robbery at a store he rarely patronized than for a customer who was shot at his regular store. They also awarded significantly higher amounts to a plane crash victim who managed to walk miles through a remote area only to die one-quarter of a mile from the nearest town than to one who traveled just as far but died seventy-five miles from the nearest town.[28] In none of the studies did the victims' losses or suffering differ based on the circumstances of their misfortunes. Nevertheless, the fate of the more highly compensated victims seemed more poignant and the victims themselves more deserving of sympathy, because subjects could more easily imagine positive outcomes for them.

A positive counterfactual also may come more easily to mind, as Delgado's examples suggest, when it is not normal for a person to suffer a particular fate. Recall the bursting of the "dot-com bubble," when unemployment figures began to reflect not just the usual losses of blue-collar and lower-skilled service jobs but also substantial losses of high-paying, white-collar jobs. Numerous news articles highlighted and analyzed the trend, labeling the downturn a "white-collar recession" and sympathetically profiling the newly idle (and mostly White) college-educated professionals for whom unemployment was both a hardship and a shock. Although white-collar professionals during that period did indeed suffer higher rates of unemployment than were typical *for that group*, they were not, as many assumed, the hardest hit: the groups that "usually get clobbered"[29] by unemployment—blue-collar workers, lower-skilled workers, people of color—continued to bear disproportionately higher job losses. The misfortunes of unemployed professionals drew more attention and greater sympathy in part because, as one economist put it, "They are not the people who come right to mind when you think about the jobless."[30]

Similarly, our attention and sympathy for crime victims varies according to how accustomed we are to seeing them—or, to be more precise, people like them—suffer crime and violence. Even the same, equally appalling forms of victimization can elicit different degrees of concern depending on race and class. A couple of high-profile cases from recent years illustrate this point. Many readers will likely recall the highly publicized 1989 case of the Central Park jogger—a case so famous that this reference to its victim generally suffices to identify it. As Kimberle Crenshaw has noted, this case, which was believed at the time to have involved the gang rape and brutal beating of a White investment banker by as many as twelve Black youths,[31] drew massive, sensationalized media coverage, provoked widespread public outrage, and even prompted Donald Trump to take out "a full page ad in four New York newspapers demanding that New York 'Bring Back the Death Penalty, Bring Back Our Police.'"[32] While she does not suggest that the Central Park jogger's case did not merit great concern, Crenshaw does point out the dramatic disparity between the level of concern that case evoked and the virtual silence of the media with regard to the "twenty-eight other cases of first-degree rape or attempted rape" that were reported in New York that same week—many of which were "as horrific as the rape in Central Park,"[33] but most of which included victims who were women of color.

Similarly, the great attention paid to a more recent and perhaps equally famous case—the June 2002 abduction of Elizabeth Smart, a White teenager from an affluent Utah family—contrasted sharply with the relative lack of coverage given a similar case that same spring: the disappearance of Alexis Patterson, a seven-year-old African American girl, in April 2002. By one account, the Smart story received ten times the media coverage given Patterson's case: one thousand newspaper articles and television reports on Smart versus one hundred on Patterson.[34] Reporters, editors, and producers denied that the victims' race played any role in the amount of attention their cases received, pointing out that a number of factors distinguished them: Smart was abducted from her own bedroom in the middle of the night while Patterson disappeared during her walk to school, the police departments may have worked differently in sharing information with the media, and the Smart parents, with their "perfect" family, may have been perceived more sympathetically than the Pattersons.[35] Aside from these circumstantial differences, however, a number of journalists and commentators noted that race probably did make a difference—not because the media consciously resist reporting stories with Black victims, but because of their sense of "what makes a compelling national story."[36] What makes a compelling story, however, often correlates with race and class. As one veteran Black journalist put it bluntly, "whatever happens in a black neighborhood doesn't really surprise anybody. The public is conditioned to expect that."[37] In other words, the explanation may be simply that crime and violence are an accepted part of Black people's "rough road in life."[38] Their suffering is normal and therefore unremarkable.

Furthermore, we take for granted not just who suffers but also how their suffering plays out. That is, we become inured to misfortunes that fit a story line with which we are familiar, because the victims' experiences are hard to imagine otherwise. The more muted reactions to deaths from enemy versus friendly fire illustrate this point. Familiarity accustoms us to racial and other group-based discrimination as well, because that kind of misfortune often follows standard scripts.

In their analysis of reactions to the bombing of a synagogue in France that injured several people, social psychologists Dale T. Miller and William Turnbull pointed out that one need not embrace a discriminatory viewpoint in order to assimilate the expectation that certain harms are normal for some people but not for others:

> France's then Prime Minister publicly denounced the attack and expressed his sympathy for both the Jews who were inside the synagogue and the "innocent passersby." The Prime Minister's differentiation of the victims and innocent passersby provoked considerabl[e] outrage because many interpreted it as implying that he did not consider the Jews to be as innocent as the passersby.
>
> Certainly the term innocent has a strong moral connotation, but should we assume that the Prime Minister's remarks reflect anti-Semitism? Not necessarily. His failure to apply the term innocent to the Jews inside the synagogue may reflect the fact that his mental representation of a synagogue enabled him to mentally remove passersby from the vicinity more easily than the attending Jews. That the passersby were not the intended victims of the attack also makes their injuries less taken-for-granted and thus easier to undo mentally (although no more or less deserved) than those of the Jews. . . . What need not have been, ought not to have been.[39]

As this incident suggests, the more readily we recognize the patterns that discrimination follows, the harder it is for us to undo mentally the routine discrimination we expect and witness, the more congruous and less remarkable we find its victims' losses, and the more acceptable they become. As a result, even extreme acts of discrimination such as bias-motivated violence can play a role in normalizing discrimination to the extent that they define the expected targets for aggression and ill treatment. Observers of bias crimes understand immediately and viscerally why the victim was singled out because they recognize the pattern that such crime follows. As Iris Marion Young has explained, the social environment surrounding acts of violence, harassment, intimidation, and ridicule of particular groups makes those acts "possible and even acceptable."[40]

This pattern of acceptance also characterizes the less dramatic, more mundane types of discrimination that members of some groups experience routinely. Dorothy E. Roberts has pointed out, for example, that habitual racial profiling in law enforcement contributes to an environment in which both the imposition of physical suffering on members of certain groups and the infringement of their constitutional rights are expected and minimized. First, discriminatory targeting by law enforcement officers reinforces the perception that some groups are "second-class citizens" for whom police surveillance and even arrest are "perfectly natural." In turn, this belief promotes the view that those groups are entitled to fewer liberties and that their rights are "mere 'amenities' that may be sacrificed to protect law-abiding people." Acceptance of this view results in an environment in which a pattern of discriminatory targeting seems benign, for "when social understandings are so uncontested that they become invisible, the social meanings that arise from them appear natural."[41]

Similarly, Deseriee A. Kennedy has explained that consumer discrimination—the commercial version of racial profiling in which retail establishments single out Black and Brown shoppers for heightened surveillance and other ill treatment—also insinuates itself into our expectations of how people of color should be treated: "Everyday racism perpetuates itself—it becomes integrated into everyday situations and becomes 'part of the expected, of the unquestionable, and of what is seen as normal by the dominant group.'"[42] And as we shall see, a history of inferior care has led to the view that minorities inevitably will suffer worse health outcomes because "those people" generally don't do well.[43]

In addition to being familiar and therefore normal, our scripts, schemas, and prototypes for discrimination incorporate other factors that make discriminatory outcomes seem inevitable and lead us to take them for granted. The standard discrimination schema includes a perpetrator who intentionally targets a member of a disfavored group for ill treatment and whose intentional wrongdoing is triggered by his "taste for discrimination"—a force both irrational and outside his control. Both the assumptions that discrimination is intended and that its perpetrators are driven to it tend to make discrimination seem ineluctable, with all the implications that the appearance of immutability carries.

As Miller and Turnbull suggested with reference to the synagogue bombing, when a victim is seen as an intended target, the victim's fate is harder to undo mentally. As they also have explained, victims' losses are more easily taken for granted when the harm they suffer was required in order for the perpetrator to achieve his goals—"even when [those] goals [are] reprehensible."[44] This tendency was confirmed in yet another victim compensation study, in which subjects showed less sympathy toward and recommended less compensation for a victim whose dog was killed by a burglar when the dog's barking "threatened the burglar's mission" than when the dog was killed when no one was nearby to hear the barking.[45] It is also harder to imagine a different outcome if an actor's behavior is viewed as out of his control than when it is controllable. For example, to the extent that people accept the stereotype of a rapist as being "sex-starved, insane, or both," they have a hard time imagining him behaving differently and refraining from his attack on the victim.[46]

Taken as a whole—and as unrealistic and inaccurate as they may sometimes be—our scripts, schemas, and prototypes of discrimination lead us to take for granted and thus to accept inequitable outcomes. And by incorporating the assumptions implicit in these conceptions of discrimination, the legal model of intentional discrimination reinforces and institutionalizes this effect.

We come, in other words, to view members of certain groups as appropriate or acceptable targets for the kinds of mistreatment that we are used to seeing them suffer. Even those of us who are vulnerable to common forms of discrimination may adopt this perspective to some degree, as we shall see below. Those who do not see themselves as likely targets of discrimination, on the other hand—that is, members of typically dominant groups—may even find comfort in these patterns. One of the less noble tendencies of human beings is to gauge our own vulnerability to negative events by comparison to others—and to prefer to compare "downward," to less fortunate others. Downward social comparison gives us a favorable, self-enhancing view of ourselves, thereby reducing anxiety and improving our sense of well-being.[47] Accordingly, individuals who can distinguish themselves from potential targets are able to reap psychological benefits from drawing that distinction. To the extent that racially discriminatory patterns of mistreatment provide nontarget individuals with more vulnerable, less fortunate groups with which to compare themselves, these patterns also provide nontarget persons with a means of enhancing their positive views of themselves and the world—to see the world as safe and just and themselves as invulnerable and worthy. To the extent that viewing some groups as expected, even accepted, targets for mistreatment provides a nontarget individual with a way of differentiating herself from that victim, she may feel even more insulated from or immune to such treatment because her group identity protects her. The comfort that comes from seeing others as more vulnerable than ourselves in turn serves to reinforce the designation of those others as suitable victims.[48]

Explaining Discriminatory Outcomes

Biases in counterfactual thinking do not just mute our reactions to discrimination, but they also influence how we explain discriminatory outcomes and evaluate the behavior of others. When bad things happen, we try to explain why. If they *are* noticed, therefore, discriminatory outcomes require explanation. Causal explanations also must be developed if someone challenges an outcome in court, because discrimination cases explicitly require the fact finder to explain the contested outcome by identifying its cause: did the defendant make the challenged decision "because of" the plaintiff's race, or for some other reason?

In order to identify the cause of a negative outcome, we tend to rely spontaneously on counterfactual thinking.[49] Much like jurors addressing the legal question of "but for" causation, we imagine what the result would have been if a different sequence of events had played out, "undoing" a scenario by changing or mutating some fact or feature of the situation and projecting how the story would have ended with that change. If the imagined result is different from the actual result, then the fact that was mutated is identified as the cause of the actual outcome.[50] This analysis typically takes the form of "what if" or "if only" thinking: when I imagine myself catching the bus by mentally undoing my purchase of a newspaper ("If only I had not stopped to buy a newspaper, I would have caught the bus."), I identify my buying the newspaper as the cause of my missing the bus.

The mutability of an *outcome* influences our search for a causal explanation. As two researchers have noted, "A causal relationship is more likely to be perceived between proposed causes and outcomes when the outcomes are highly mutable. . . . [C]ounterfactual thinking would not support a causal link between failing to carry an umbrella and a rainstorm, because the rainstorm is an immutable event."[51] In other words, unlike "if only" thinking, counterfactual thinking that takes the form of an "even if" statement—"even if I had brought an umbrella, it would have rained"—would not supply a causal explanation for the outcome. The expectation that certain groups will suffer certain kinds of misfortunes thus may prevent us both from reacting to those outcomes *and* from questioning how they materialize.

Likewise, an *antecedent event* will not be identified as having caused the outcome unless it is psychologically mutable. Social psychologists have pointed out, for example, that, "following a suicide in which a man leapt from a window, people would not cite the presence of gravity as a cause of his death. Although it is true that an absence of gravity would have undone the outcome, the presence of gravity is an immutable characteristic of life on Earth."[52] Conversely, the more mutable the antecedent event, the greater its presumed causality. Therefore, the greater the ease with which we can picture an actor doing something differently, with a different (more positive) result, the greater the responsibility and blame we will assign that person for the bad thing that actually happened. Even random features of an event can lead us to assess blame differently if they make an event more or less easy to mentally undo. In the burglar study, for example, not only were his victims viewed with greater sympathy, but the burglar who struck the night before the victims returned from vacation was judged more harshly than the burglar who broke in weeks earlier.[53]

When more than one actor plays a part in a situation that has a negative outcome, the person whose behavior is most readily mutated will tend to be assigned the most responsibility and blame for the outcome. Much as the difficulty or ease of imagining alternatives distorts our emotional reactions to negative events, the perceived mutability of the parties' behavior can have a perverse effect on our explanations of them. It sometimes results, for example, in our assigning an undue degree of blame to the victim of a crime for his or her own victimization. As two commentators put it:

> [D]escriptions of a harmful act often present the actions of the perpetrator in a way that makes him or her part of the presupposed background of the story and, as such, relatively immutable. With the victim's actions perceived as more mutable than those of the perpetrator, counterfactual scenarios in which harm is avoided will tend to be ones that change the victim's past actions but keep the aggressor's behavior essentially constant. The higher availability of counterfactual scenarios that modify the victim's actions, in turn, may induce an impression that the victim is responsible for his or her fate.[54]

The influence of perceived mutability may not result in the perpetrator entirely escaping blame. It can, however, lead observers to question the victim's behavior and reduce the amount of responsibility they place on the perpetrator. As a result, "People may say of a rape 'Of course, he is to blame.' but go on to say 'But why didn't she do X?' or 'If only she had done X and not Y.'"[55]

Another important influence on the way we assign responsibility is our preference for the normal or customary—a preference that makes it difficult for us to imagine alternatives to behavior to which we are accustomed. Because of this preference, we tend to assign less responsibility for a bad result to an actor who behaves consistently with normal patterns, because it is harder to imagine him acting differently.[56] Recent studies confirmed the cognitive effect of the normality bias on legal decision making through experiments that examined mock jurors' judgments of causation, blame, compensation, and punishment.[57] These studies tested jurors' assessments of defendants' behavior in experiments that centered around a medical malpractice claim and an investment loss. In each experiment, jurors were presented with either a normal or an abnormal scenario: in the medical malpractice case the defendant doctor treated the patient with either a conventional (normal) or an unconventional (abnormal) protocol, and in the investment case the defendant financial adviser placed the client's inheritance in either "widely owned conventional stocks" (normal) or "less widely owned unconventional stocks" (abnormal). Jurors were significantly more likely to find fault with the defendant's conduct and to determine that it caused the plaintiff's death or loss when the defendant's treatment or investment choice was unconventional than when it was conventional. In the medical malpractice case, jurors also were more likely to find that the defendant deserved substantial blame and bore a heavy moral responsibility when he chose an unconventional treatment. Their decisions on liability and compensation reflected these views as well, by favoring the plaintiffs more when the defendant acted unconventionally.

Based on these results, the studies' authors propose that "blame and punishment are closely linked to perceptions of abnormality. Those who violate norms . . . incur greater responsibility for subsequent outcomes than those who tread along well-established paths."[58] They offer a couple of explanations for why these jurors were, as people generally are, easier on those who follow well-worn paths and harder on those who stake out new ones. First, our strong preference for preserving and reinforcing that which we see as normal causes us to find it difficult to blame people who behave "in ways that preserve, rather than undermine, the social order,"[59] for "it is hard for us to see negative agency in normal conduct."[60] Indeed, we may even want to commend their actions, for "to be normal is to be acceptable, right, and in step with the world."[61] Conversely, we find it easier to blame those who defy convention when things go wrong both because it is easier to imagine them making a different choice and because they have violated a social norm and thereby threatened the social order.

Our preference for conformity to and compliance with expectations carries through to the way we direct and evaluate our own behavior as well. This is another reason why, as we saw earlier, situational pressures can lead us to behave badly—for example, to refrain from helping a person in need if everyone else is ignoring his plight—despite our better natures.[62]

"Acceptable, Right, and in Step with the World"

The second-guessing of the victim's behavior, and comparative acceptance of the perpetrator's, also appears in our evaluations of the perpetrator and target of discrimination. Again our scripts, schemas, and prototypes distort our assessments, because our assumptions about the forces that produce discrimination lead us to view discrimination as inevitable and, accordingly, the perpetrator's actions as immutable. In particular, the assumptions that perpetrators are irrational and driven by distaste for the targeted group contribute to a reduction in the degree of responsibility they bear for their behavior. While we may condemn that behavior and their presumed motivations, we also relieve perpetrators of full responsibility to the extent that we believe it would be futile to try to deter or change them (whether by punishing them or holding them liable for the harm they cause) or regard them with a shrugging acceptance.

Perpetrators of both extreme and ordinary forms of discrimination benefit from this tendency. Opponents of bias crime legislation, for example, have contended that hate crime perpetrators are "not fully responsible for" their prejudice and should not be punished more severely on account of it.[63] Similarly, the prototypical "racist cop" who deliberately sets out to harass minorities may be viewed as uncontrollable and unchangeable.[64] And a sense of resignation and even tolerance is evident in the common reaction to young men who assault gays and women: "Boys will be boys."[65] We also reduce the responsibility we place on perpetrators of run-of-the-mill discrimination to the extent that we assume that they, like those who commit more extreme acts, are driven by an irrational, character-based aversion to people from certain groups.[66] If the actor discriminates because he has a defective character, it is hard to imagine him acting differently, so we regard his behavior as unchangeable, resign ourselves to it, and focus our inquiry instead on how the victim could have avoided the bad outcome.

Our preference for conventional behavior also reduces the responsibility we place on those who discriminate. To the extent that certain discriminatory practices have become routine, therefore, individuals who follow them may be insulated from blame. In less threatening or more mundane situations, where many discriminatory practices are so well established that we take them for granted, we are especially prone to minimize the behavior of someone who discriminates and to focus unduly on what the victim might have done to invite such treatment.

In some ways, it only seems fair to reduce the responsibility we place on someone who follows standard practice. After all, practices *become* standard based on the actions of many, and it hardly seems reasonable to hold one unlucky practitioner responsible for doing what others traditionally have done with impunity, especially considering the patina of legitimacy that the practice has thereby acquired. As David Harris has pointed out, the "great majority of police officers" who make use of racial profiling "do so not because they are bigoted or bad, but because they think it is the right way to catch criminals. Racial profiling is an institutional practice—a tactic accepted and encouraged by police agencies as a legitimate, effective crime-fighting tool."[67]

But while we may sympathize with the individual who follows standard practice, we also should recognize that our preference for the existing order carries disturbing implications. Because it insulates from scrutiny practices that are common and have come to be expected, it also may lead us to overlook the deficiencies of standard practices. In other words, because our assessments are biased in favor of the routine and expected, we equate "normal" with "appropriate" and even "desirable."

As Harris explains, until the use of racial profiling in law enforcement recently came under critical scrutiny it had long enjoyed the presumption of legitimacy. Courts regularly deferred to officers' judgments to question, detain, and search individuals based on race or ethnicity, thereby elevating the practice to a kind of expertise.[68] In many cases, however, what the courts, the police, and the general public viewed as an expert's well-considered judgment was actually based on no more than "a kind of folk wisdom—information that has more in common with stories and legends than with well-constructed patterns of data."[69] But because the practice was so well established, and therefore was assumed to be rational and effective, it went "untested, unexamined, and unchallenged" for many years.[70]

When critics subjected racial profiling to empirical analysis, their studies revealed that this standard practice could not withstand rigorous statistical scrutiny. They found, for example, that racial profiling was *not* improving law enforcement "hit rates"—"the rates at which police actually find contraband or other evidence of crime when they perform stops and searches."[71] Instead, in several jurisdictions where minorities were stopped or searched at rates greatly exceeding those of Whites, hit rates for minorities were about the same as or even lower than those for Whites. Racial profiling therefore did not fulfill the only potential justification for the practice: that it would improve law enforcement by helping officers to catch criminals.[72] Indeed, and as Harris also points out, the very statistical foundation on which racial profiling rests—the higher arrest and incarceration rates among Blacks, Latinos, and other minorities as compared to Whites—is itself the product of racially biased law enforcement policies that create a self-fulfilling prophecy that falsely confirms a biased expectation equating race and criminality.[73]

Furthermore, by insulating this flawed practice from scrutiny, the presumption of legitimacy accorded racial profiling does not just mask its methodological failings but also distorts the cost-benefit analysis by which we evaluate it. First, the presumption of legitimacy inflates the value of a benefit that turns out to be illusory. But beyond distorting the positive side of the trade-off, ready acceptance of racial profiling also prevents us from taking a hard look at the full range of its costs. For one thing, misplaced faith in the effectiveness of racial profiling casts as illegitimate the complaints of those who bear its most direct burdens: the many innocent individuals who are inconvenienced, humiliated, placed in mortal fear, and sometimes subjected to physical injury solely on the basis of their skin color or ethnic appearance. As we have seen in the period since 9/11, a time that has sparked renewed calls for racial and ethnic profiling, even members of some groups that are vulnerable to racial profiling have argued that their group should bear this cost—indeed, should *welcome* the chance to be profiled—if it will prevent another 9/11.[74]

Such a view tends to discount the true costs of racial profiling: not only are the burdens borne by *targets* more onerous and extensive than might be readily apparent, but the costs of racial profiling do not end with the individual targets. Ultimately, all of us bear them.

Whether or not they personally are stopped or searched, members of commonly targeted groups bear the costs of racial profiling when efforts to *avoid* being detained become a part of their daily routines. For example, to minimize their chances of being noticed or stopped by police, or to decrease the likelihood that they will be treated abusively if they are, Black and Latino motorists may adjust numerous aspects of their daily lives.

> These adjustments may include driving cars that are bland and not "flashy," dressing in drab clothing or avoiding accessories that

> might make them noticeable, sitting erect at all times while driving, obtaining "vanity" license plates that advertise their educational degrees or professional status, keeping the radio tuned to a classical music station, and scheduling extra time for car trips to allow for the delay involved in a traffic stop.[75]

They may also include staying out of predominantly White neighborhoods altogether.[76] This sense of responsibility for avoiding abusive treatment from police passes from one generation to the next when young Black males receive "The Lesson" or "The Talk": instructions from their elders on "how to behave when—not if—they are stopped by police."[77]

Members of targeted groups also suffer, as we have seen, when widespread acceptance of racial profiling leads us to regard it as normal, because that view promotes the expectation that people who look like them naturally will be watched and stopped, as well as the understanding that their rights, liberty, and bodily integrity have less value than others'.

What those of us who do not consider ourselves vulnerable to racial profiling (as well as some of us who do) may fail to realize, however, is that the practice imposes costs on everyone. Racial profiling contributes to the racial division of our society because it limits the mobility of racial minorities and thereby "reinforces existing segregation in housing and employment."[78] Simply put, the need to contend with racial profiling is a strong disincentive for racial minorities to move into or travel through predominantly White areas, so many people of color will avoid doing so. (Ironically—but not surprisingly, given the power of expectations to shape environments—the more segregated our spaces are, the more likely it is that a person of color will seem out of place in a designated "White" neighborhood, and the more likely that person is to be viewed as suspicious and potentially criminal.[79] Even driving a bland car at a sane rate of speed while listening to Brahms on the radio may not help.)

Finally, racially biased law enforcement practices work against the interests of criminal justice and public safety because they are counterproductive. They undermine the legitimacy of the legal system and place a barrier between the police and the people who are most likely to be able to help them prevent and solve crimes. In surveys of public opinion, high percentages of respondents from racial minority groups—and substantial percentages of Whites as well—report that they believe the police treat people unfairly because of race.[80] Many also report that they mistrust the police and would be less likely to believe a police officer's testimony in court.[81] As Harris notes, these views create skepticism about the legitimacy of courts and their decisions, and they also have more immediate, practical consequences for the ability of police officers to perform their duties. Citizens' mistrust of the police stands in the way of the relationships with those citizens that the police need in order to make effective use of promising new policing methods, such as community-oriented policing. That mistrust also leads jurors in criminal cases to disbelieve or dismiss the testimony of police officers—often the most important, or even the only, witnesses for the prosecution—thereby frustrating the system's ability to keep real criminals off the streets.[82]

Racial profiling in law enforcement is an obvious, but not the only, example of how differential treatment based on race or ethnicity comes to be viewed as appropriate and thereby to escape both sanction and careful examination. As we shall see, the use of race as a diagnostic factor in health care, which has been likened to racial profiling, has become a standard practice as well—one that is passed from one generation of physicians to the next as part of medicine's "silent curriculum." Like racial profiling in law enforcement, this practice raises concerns about its equity and its effectiveness. And as racial profiling had until it came under closer scrutiny, race-based medicine enjoys a presumption of legitimacy as part of a culture in which thinking about patients in terms of race is both expected and unnoticed—simply "the way that it is done."[83] As a result, a physician's adherence to race-based standard practices does not just tend to absolve her of responsibility for the discriminatory effects of those practices but is regarded as normal protocol.

It is not just practices like these, arising in a professional setting and with the veneer of expertise, that benefit from a preference for the normal. Even acts that few would regard as proper may be viewed as less culpable if they follow a familiar pattern. For example, when antigay violence follows the standard script for gay bashing—a group of young men or boys assaulting a gay man or boy—elders and law enforcement officials often minimize the perpetrators' acts, viewing them not as a hate crime but as a rite of passage. For some young males, that is, joining in such an attack is a way *to be accepted* by their peers and by society.[84] Violence against or harassment of women too is often regarded as a normal, socially acceptable, and even a recreational activity for men, and likewise may provide its male perpetrators with a way to bond and achieve social status.[85]

When it comes to assessing legal responsibility, the normality bias benefits defendants in two ways. First, some legal standards for liability explicitly adopt a preference for the customary, so to the extent the defendant was following a standard practice he is more likely to be absolved of wrongdoing. For example, if a defendant's culpability is assessed by reference to an appropriate standard of care, as in a medical malpractice case, his adherence to customary medical practices, even those that incorporate race as a diagnostic factor, will be a strong factor in his defense.[86]

Second, and as the studies discussed earlier suggest, juries may be highly susceptible to persuasion through arguments that employ counterfactual thinking. *Both* plaintiffs' and defendants' lawyers can make use of counterfactual thinking in the narratives they construct for their cases (a point that will be examined later), but defense lawyers may be more savvy at exploiting this potential. Of course, the defense already benefits from the general tendency to view the perpetrator's behavior as an unalterable part of the background and the victim's as correspondingly more mutable. In addition, in some cases the legal elements of the claim direct the fact finder's attention to the victim's behavior. In sexual harassment or assault cases, for example, the jury commonly must determine whether the victim welcomed or consented to the defendant's behavior.[87] (As we will see, our stereotypes and cultural scripts for these situations may reinforce the legal focus on and tendency to blame the victim.)[88] But even these advantages can be improved on, and defense lawyers commonly employ a couple of techniques to beneficial effect.

One is to portray the defendant and his actions as utterly ordinary and conventional, thereby triggering the normality bias. A defense lawyer could portray a police officer who disproportionately targets racial and ethnic minorities as acting on "intuition and experience"[89]—that is, as just following sound police practices that happen to have "an unfortunate byproduct."[90] And again, even perpetrators of extreme acts can be presented as normal. In gay-bashing cases, for example, "a common defense strategy is to portray the perpetrator as an 'average' person whose 'actions are neither serious nor unusual,' through, for example, evidence of '"good family background, exemplary behavior in school, and participation in organized athletics.'"[91]

Another tactic is to portray the victim's behavior as highly controllable, by presenting the jury with various counterfactual scenarios in which the plaintiff behaved differently and, consequently, escaped harm. In sexual harassment or assault cases, for example, the defense attorney might suggest several things the plaintiff could have done differently—not dressed suggestively, not flirted with the defendant, not accepted his invitation to join him for a drink—that could have prevented or put a stop to the defendant's advances.[92] As we shall see, placing the focus on the victim creates another opening for counterfactual thinking to reinforce existing, biased norms.

"If Only" Counterfactuals and Blaming the Victim

Our evaluations of victim behavior may reinforce our acceptance of discriminatory outcomes. We may not fully absolve perpetrators of discrimination for their actions. For example, even those who oppose enhanced punishment for bias crimes agree that the perpetrator should be blamed for the underlying crime.[93] At the same time, however, the perceived inevitability of their conduct leads us to accept the pattern it follows—and to assume the victim should have, too. And, as we have seen, the comparative immutability of the perpetrator's behavior and mutability of the victim's divert us from scrutinizing the actions of the perpetrator and focus us instead on what the victim might have done differently to avoid being targeted.[94]

This bias in perceived mutability dovetails with another psychological bias that actually *motivates* us to blame the victim of a negative event: the general tendency and desire to believe that the world makes sense. This general belief comprises three specific suppositions about the world: that it is just and orderly, that it is meaningful, and that it is controllable: "People deserve what they get and get what they deserve,"[95] bad things will not happen to people of good moral character, and people can control their environment through their behavior.[96] These beliefs influence our reactions to victims of negative events, because we prefer to explain those events in a way that allows us to preserve our belief in a just and meaningful world and our feelings of invulnerability and control. Our self-interest is served, therefore, if we can differentiate ourselves from the victim by viewing the victim as having caused his own misfortune. Even people who suffer extreme mistreatment are not immune from scrutiny. For example, the general tendency to blame victims of crime for inviting their own misfortune has been well documented and analyzed.[97] We may identify actions the victim took that contributed to the bad outcome or, if we can find nothing in the victim's behavior that could have caused the event, we may even derogate the victim's character by seeing him as "the sort of person who deserved to be victimized"[98]—in other words, as a suitable victim.

Accordingly, victims who are targeted for violence or abuse based upon their membership in a socially vulnerable group often are blamed for their own victimization. Because they should have recognized, as everyone else does, that their very identities mark them as potential targets, they may be held responsible based on such seemingly unobjectionable behavior as being visible, traveling beyond their usual orbit, dressing attractively, or asserting their rights. Observers might, for example, blame the victim of antigay violence for having hung out in a place, worn flamboyant clothing, or behaved in a way that made his sexual orientation "obvious."[99] A woman who is harassed in a public place might also be questioned as to what she was doing there or what she was wearing.[100] When a Black person is attacked while walking in a White neighborhood, observers may ask what the victim was doing in that neighborhood to begin with. As Patricia Williams wrote following the 1986 Howard Beach incident:

> A veritable Greek chorus formed, comprised of the defendants' lawyers and resident after resident after resident of Howard Beach, all repeating and repeating and repeating that the mere presence of three black men in that part of town at that time of night was reason enough to drive them out. "They had to be starting trouble." "We're strictly a white neighborhood." "What were they doing here in the first place?"[101]

The evaluation of a victim's behavior also provides another occasion for the reinforcement of stereotypes. In general, our preference for the normal leads us to resist and even to penalize individuals whose behavior is out of step with or challenges the existing order. Because it is easier to mentally undo behavior that is considered atypical or abnormal, a person who behaves inconsistently with expectations invites criticism and blame if a negative outcome follows.[102]

Even if a person merely acts in a way that is out of character *for him*, he may be assigned greater responsibility if he thereafter suffers a bad outcome.[103] This may be the case even when the atypical behavior did nothing to increase the foreseeability or probability of the bad result. In one study, for example, the actions of a driver who got into an accident while taking an unusual route home were perceived as more causal than the actions of a driver who suffered an accident on his usual way home, even where the route taken had no effect on the probability or foreseeability of the accident.[104] Because subjects could more easily imagine the former driver avoiding the accident, they viewed him as playing a greater role in causing it.

Whether or not a person's behavior conforms to group-based stereotypes also affects its mutability, because behavior that is inconsistent with stereotypes tends to be viewed as exceptional and therefore abnormal. As a result, victims who act contrary to stereotypical expectations tend to be judged as more responsible for their fates, and the perpetrator accordingly as less. This tendency can lead to the perverse judgment that the victim "deserved" her misfortune.

In one set of studies, for example, subjects reached paradoxical judgments of rape victims and their attackers when the victims behaved inconsistently with gender stereotypes.[105] In those studies, subjects assigned greater responsibility for their own rapes to rape victims who strongly resisted their attackers by using high levels of both vocal and physical resistance than to victims who resisted less strongly. When the women resisted strongly, subjects also were less sure of the guilt of the rapist and recommended that he receive a shorter sentence. One subject's response to the high resistance scenario employed textbook counterfactual thinking: "If she had not been so rudely aggressive she might not have been raped."[106]

The studies' authors pointed out the paradox in these judgments: on one hand, a woman who resists is viewed favorably because people believe that potential rape victims should resist. First, resisting may be an effective way to avoid being raped and second, if she is unable to fend off her attacker, the victim's resistance provides evidence that she did not consent to sexual contact and was indeed raped. (Accordingly, subjects in the study questioned whether victims who resisted very little had been raped.) On the other hand, a woman who resists invites disapproval as well, because showing strong resistance is inconsistent with the stereotype of women as passive, compliant, submissive, and weak. As a result of these opposing effects, "there is a fine line that a victim must not cross."[107] She must resist exactly the right amount—enough to convince jurors that she did not consent, but not so much as to be unladylike—in order to be absolved of responsibility for causing the attack and in order for the rapist to be seen as fully responsible.

While the rape study provides an especially vivid example of how our evaluations of victims can serve as a way of policing adherence to norms, the study's authors point out that it is just one illustration of a common phenomenon by which people face penalties for behaving in ways that are unexpected, unusual, or stereotype-inconsistent. As we have seen, women who assert themselves by taking on leadership roles may elicit nonverbal, perhaps unconscious, expressions of disapproval from observers who may not even realize that they expect women to behave in a less assertive, more stereotype-compliant manner.[108] Whether or not the observers appreciate the effect of gender stereotypes on their reactions, their unconscious bias leads them, along with other members of their team, to view *the very same contribution* as less valuable when it is made by a woman than when it is made by a man. Presumably, these reactions are cumulative over time, and if that woman were later passed over for a promotion she might find it difficult to prove that she was a victim of gender discrimination because "objective" evaluations of her work might support the employer's decision. Thus, in addition to setting off a self-fulfilling prophecy, gender stereotypes can enforce and reinforce the view that it is not normal for women to take leadership positions.

Living by "Normal"

When we judge people against a standard of "normal," we exert pressure on them to live by that standard. That is, our reactions to and explanations of their outcomes both police and broadcast our definitions of appropriate conduct and social conditions. And it is not just observers who exhibit these normality-biased reactions or develop normality-biased explanations; the individuals who are the focus of those reactions and explanations may respond that way as well.

Targets and potential targets of discrimination are equally familiar with the standard scripts for discrimination and, like everyone else, we may accept them as a given—part of the background against which we travel. To the extent that we see that background as immutable, we too may focus our efforts to avoid victimization on the one aspect that we are able to control: our own behavior. Accordingly, those of us who are vulnerable to discrimination may accept responsibility for our own victimization by adopting various strategies for negotiating a world in which discrimination is a real and constant force. Those strategies might, ironically, make us complicit in our own subordination by leading us to act in ways that reinforce stereotypes and other biased expectations because those types of behavior make us seem more normal.

We have already seen the various measures that drivers of color adopt to avoid drawing the attention of law enforcement officers. Minorities can deploy similar strategies to avoid other types of mistreatment. To avoid being targeted for a hate crime, for example, members of socially vulnerable groups might avoid going to places where they might "stick out," or decline to engage in activities that might draw attention to them. Some writers have described how their fear of hate crime has influenced even such seemingly mundane decisions as what neighborhoods to drive or run through, what events to attend, and even what vacation spots to patronize.[109] Another strategy may be to engage in behavior that is expected—that is, stereotypical of one's social group—so as to avoid attracting unwanted attention. For example, someone who fears antigay harassment or violence might feel compelled to behave in rigidly defined, stereotypically gendered ways: "men might not touch other men; women might not excel at tasks that require physical exertion."[110]

Behaving in a stereotype-consistent, "normal" way may benefit individuals in other ways as well, by helping someone who views herself as vulnerable to discrimination to avoid other kinds of negative treatment or to find favor. As we have seen, one factor that contributes to the behavioral confirmation of stereotypes in social interactions is that people often comply with stereotypical expectations in order to gain the approval of someone else who expects or demands such a response—or at least to avoid their disapproval. People might avoid rejection in a broader sense by sticking to activities that seem stereotype-consistent as well. For example, Asian Americans might "confine themselves, perhaps unconsciously, to the roles that whites are more likely to find acceptable," by, for example, gravitating toward "the math, science, and engineering fields," in part as "a mechanism for coping with anticipated rejection" and as a way of minimizing their susceptibility to racial bias.[111]

Obviously, strategies of this kind do nothing to challenge, and much to reinforce, our biased expectations. Beyond that, they also contribute to our general inability to see the connection between that bias and the disparate outcomes that materialize, because they make stereotypical expectations normal, immutable, and ultimately, invisible.

5

Discrimination by and as Default in Medical Care

We have seen the difficulty of identifying cases in which discriminatory treatment has *occurred*—not to speak of determining whether it was *intended*—because the same situations that tend to promote discriminatory behavior also tend to obscure it. We also have seen that it is difficult to discern discriminatory outcomes because they fit so well with our view of what is normal. As a result, discrimination is the default setting to which our actions and outcomes are inclined, and, like many other kinds of defaults, once it is set we tend neither to notice it nor to exert the effort to change it. These points have important implications in situations that are characterized by normative ambiguity, conditions that promote rather than disrupt the behavioral confirmation of expectations, and standard practices that establish disparate outcomes as normal. The worst such settings would be those in which decision making is complex and subjective (and, accordingly, in which decision makers tend to be granted a great deal of discretion and deference), race- or other group-based expectations are institutionally accepted and reinforced, and decision makers have greater power than the subjects of their decisions but lack the incentive or resources to disrupt the influence of erroneous expectations on their behavior and decisions.

Medical care is one setting that is characterized by all these factors and in which the potential for *racial* bias, in particular, has received great attention recently. We know that substantial race-based disparities in health care status and medical treatment exist, because they have been documented. On the other hand, pinpointing the cause, or even identifying the existence, of racial bias in an individual case is a more complex and controversial proposition. One generalization that can be asserted with some confidence, however, is that it is not so much the "person" (that is, the medical decision maker) as it is the situation that produces the large share of racial disparities in medical care. As medical professionals, social scientists, and legal scholars have shown, the medical decision-making environment is shaped by conditions that promote racial bias, including institutional knowledge, practices, and constraints that channel medical decision makers to think in terms of race—and patients, sometimes, to respond accordingly.

Racial Disparities in Medical Outcomes and Treatment

Recent statistics document significant differences in mortality and health status between Blacks and Whites.[1] Those numbers show, for example, that Blacks have a shorter life expectancy and higher death rate, higher rate of infant mortality, and higher prevalence of many diseases than Whites.[2] Moreover, numerous studies indicate that patients from racial and ethnic minority groups receive an inferior level of medical care compared to White patients. While these differences may take the form of "more" or "less" care for Blacks as compared with Whites, the real issue is that the disparities suggest that "minorities may have health care services *poorly matched* to their needs."[3] For example, African American patients tend to undergo fewer expensive or advanced medical procedures and to receive a lower level of pain relief than Whites, while also being subjected more frequently to medical hardships, such as amputations.[4] In addition, Black patients with psychiatric disorders often are given more severe diagnoses and prescribed more restrictive treatment than White patients exhibiting similar symptoms, or, alternatively, are not treated for their mental illness because they are misdiagnosed as having substance abuse problems.[5]

Many experts believe that at least part of this disparity can be attributed to racial bias in the delivery of medical care. For example, in its 2002 report, *Unequal Treatment: Confronting Racial and Ethnic Disparities in Health Care*, the Institute of Medicine concluded that "[b]ias, stereotyping, prejudice, and clinical uncertainty on the part of health care providers may contribute to racial and ethnic disparities in healthcare" and called for "greater understanding" of and research into "the prevalence and influence of these processes."[6] Other prominent physicians and organizations have expressed similar concerns.[7] Some commentators, on the other hand, have asserted that the focus on physician bias is itself "divisive" and "worrisome,"[8] or that more important explanations for racial disparities lie elsewhere, such as in differential resources and access to health care[9] or differential patient preferences.[10]

Undoubtedly, a complicated set of factors plays a role in producing disparities in health care and outcomes. Disparities in access and resources alone do not account for the documented inequalities in health status, however, for racially disparate outcomes persist even when studies control for access to health care and socioeconomic status.[11] Nor can an explanation based in patient preferences be viewed as negating that of racial bias in treatment. Proponents of the "patient preference" explanation suggest that patients' own cultural preferences play a role in health disparities, for some members of groups receiving inferior care may prefer the types of treatment they receive.[12] To be sure, patients' preferences generally should be taken into account in prescribing treatment, and patients may decline to submit to particular interventions for a range of reasons, such as cultural beliefs favoring nontraditional treatment or individual aversion to risky or invasive procedures. Yet patient preference cannot be considered a sound *alternative* explanation for racial disparities, for it ignores the potential for racial bias on the part of the physician to influence the patient's view of his or her choices. In other words, and as will be examined further below, differential patient preferences may in some cases constitute another example of a self-fulfilling prophecy that provides false confirmation of the expectation of difference.

Further, some patient "preferences" are themselves a product of race discrimination. They may, for example, be a reaction to the patient's experience or expectation of being treated poorly within a biased system and reflect the patient's mistrust of health care professionals.[13] Their awareness of the history of racial discrimination in medicine—including medical experimentation and other discriminatory practices—may lead Black patients to fear abuse or to feel an aversion toward aggressive treatment. As one legal scholar has explained, this cycle may be self-perpetuating:

> [T]he history of racial abuses in American medicine may have had the effect of putting into motion a vicious cycle: The history of discrimination causes blacks, as a group, to distrust white doctors; because blacks distrust doctors, they are generally more likely to decline aggressive or risky medical treatment; since blacks as a group are more likely to decline aggressive treatments, doctors (employing stereotypes) assume that individual black patients will prefer less aggressive treatment; and because doctors make this assumption, they are less likely to offer aggressive treatment to their black patients.[14]

Differential preferences also may mirror racial disparities in treatment. Some studies have traced differential preferences to differences in patterns of referral for treatment or to perceived chances of positive outcome. For example, Black patients sometimes are not referred as frequently as Whites for advanced procedures or are referred at a later point in their illness, when the suggested procedure is less likely to be helpful.[15] Other studies have found that patients' resistance to a proposed treatment sometimes is based in a lack of familiarity with procedures that may be related to race. That is, patients are disinclined to agree to procedures that have not been explained to them, and sometimes patients of color do not receive the relevant information.[16] Alternatively, resistance to a course of treatment may reflect the patient's belief that the suggested procedures tend to result in greater complications for patients in communities that receive a lower level of care. Thus, "patient 'preference' for less intensive treatment may in fact represent resignation to the perceived status quo—that interventions are unavailable, unaffordable, ineffective, or unduly risky—even if those perceptions are not accurate."[17]

Moreover, to assert that racial bias influences the delivery of health care is not to suggest that individual medical professionals intentionally deliver inferior care to people of color. Those who cite bias as a cause of disparate outcomes have been careful to explain that inequities in health care cannot, for the most part, be attributed to individual, ill-intentioned "perpetrators" and can occur despite individual practitioners' good intentions.[18] While some individual practitioners may intend to discriminate, that is not thought to be a significant explanation for racial disparities in health care.[19] In the health care context, no less than in other areas of life, racial discrimination can best be understood as a product of the "symbiotic relationship" among a number of forces. The medical context is characterized by factors that both promote and obscure the influence of racial bias, such that "racial profiling"[20] can occur "unreflectively, even unconsciously, as a matter of routine"[21]—that is, by default.

Channeling Racially Disparate Care: Institutional and Cognitive Influences on Medical Decision Making

In some ways, medical care in this country is set up to allow a patient's race to influence diagnosis and treatment. Medical institutions themselves actually reward and perpetuate race-based diagnosis and treatment when they transmit and sustain the view that race is an important, "natural," scientific category, and therefore a relevant factor in health care through a number of standard practices. For example, a doctor presenting a case to colleagues is expected to identify the patient's race and will be questioned for failing to do so.[22] This practice, along with "a mixed bag of notions, views and attitudes" about correlations between race and disease, are part of the "silent curriculum" that is transmitted from each generation of practitioners to the next,[23] and contributes to a culture in which thinking about patients in terms of race has become both expected and invisible—simply "the way that it is done."[24]

René Bowser has argued forcefully that the idea that race is relevant was created, and continues to be developed and transmitted, through medical research that uses race as a variable, linking race to biological difference and perpetuating the notion that biological inferiority, rather than other factors such as differences in resources or care, accounts for the inferior health outcomes of Blacks.[25] (Some have argued, on the other hand, that including race as a variable in medical research is an important means of identifying the role that racial discrimination plays in producing health disparities. One scholar argues that race-related medical data are needed in order to "monitor progress or setbacks" in addressing inequalities. He also warns, however, that "[w]e must be cautious . . . in our use of race as a variable, taking care to define what race means in our research, avoiding assumptions of biological differences, and accounting for distinctions between race and socioeconomic status.")[26]

The tradition of racialized medical research had shameful origins, having begun with an agenda to justify slavery[27] and having included the use of African Americans as "clinical material in teaching and research"[28]—perhaps the most famous example of such being the Tuskegee syphilis experiment of 1932–1972.[29] The Tuskegee Study, perhaps more than any other event, has engendered widespread and lasting feelings of distrust of the medical community among African Americans.[30] In a 2002–2003 telephone survey of African Americans' viewpoints, up to 60 percent of respondents agreed with specific conspiracy beliefs about the role of the government or health care system in creating HIV or preventing the cure of AIDS, conditions that disproportionately affect African Americans. While relatively low percentages agreed with the most extreme statements—only 12 percent believed that

"HIV was created and spread by the CIA," and 16.2 percent that "AIDS was created by the government to control the black population"—significant proportions of respondents agreed with statements suggesting that the system either is indifferent to African Americans or is experimenting on them. For example, 58.8 percent agreed with the statement, "A lot of information about AIDS is being held back from the public," 53.4 percent agreed that "There is a cure for AIDS, but it is being withheld from the poor," and 43.6 percent agreed that "People who take the new medicines for HIV are human guinea pigs for the government."[31] The history of race and medicine also includes the racial segregation of medical care and the outright denial of medical care to Black people.[32]

But that history has largely been overlooked or forgotten, and the belief that Blacks are biologically, as well as culturally, different from Whites has become part of the unquestioned, "background" knowledge of the profession.[33] "Evidence" derived from such research is incorporated into "racial profiles" on which doctors may, consciously or not, rely in making decisions about diagnosis and treatment. These profiles include the assumptions that Blacks are genetically predisposed to certain diseases, better able to tolerate pain and suffering, and culturally disinclined to take an active role in their health care or to comply with treatment plans.[34] As commentators have noted, medical decisions that rely on race as a diagnostic factor when it may not be warranted nevertheless contribute to the perpetuation of racial profiles in medicine by creating a self-fulfilling prophecy whereby physicians' racially biased diagnoses are incorporated into epidemiological data that, in turn, are used as objective, empirical "evidence" of race-related biological difference.[35]

These racial profiles, coupled with practitioners' own racial biases, potentially play a large role in medical decision making. There is no reason to think that medical professionals are immune to the influence of racial and other group-based stereotypes that affect everyone else, and good reason to believe both that such stereotypes do influence doctors' perceptions of patients and that these stereotypes affect the quality of care they deliver.[36] Although, consistent with professional ideals, physicians had long denied being influenced by patients' personal characteristics in their interactions with or treatment decisions for them, several studies over the past few decades have found that medical professionals do in fact behave differently with different patients. Studies have found, for example, that physicians, nurses, and medical students evaluate or treat patients differently based on such characteristics as the patient's physical appearance (such as body weight), perceived "social worth" (such as the extent to which the patient is seen as contributing to society), age, disability, sexual orientation, and perceived deviance (such as alcoholism).[37]

In one recent study, doctors themselves reported having more negative perceptions of their African American patients than of their White patients.[38] The doctors in this study (all cardiac care physicians and most of them White)[39] reported that they regarded their African American patients as less intelligent, less educated, and less rational than their White patients. They also expected their African American patients to be less likely than their White patients to participate in cardiac rehabilitation or to comply with medical advice, but more likely than the White patients to abuse alcohol or other drugs. In addition, the doctors expressed lesser feelings of "affiliation" toward their African American patients, for they less frequently rated them as being "very pleasant" or expressed feeling about them that "[t]his patient is the kind of person I can see myself being friends with." Attitudes such as these, whether explicit or implicit,[40] can lead to an "attenuation of empathy across racial lines" that leads to the "unconscious devaluation of minority patients' hopes, fears, and life prospects."[41]

For some patients, physicians' negative race-based expectations merge with similarly negative perceptions of patients who are poor or not well educated, because race is highly correlated with socioeconomic status.[42] In the study of cardiac care physicians' race-based perceptions, the researchers analyzed separately whether doctors' attitudes were influenced by patients' income and education levels. While results did not differ for patients in the middle and highest socioeconomic status groups, patients in the lowest socioeconomic status group did fare worse in physicians' assessments: the doctors were more likely to perceive those patients as being dependent, irresponsible, irrational, and unintelligent. They also viewed the patients of lower socioeconomic status as being less likely to participate in cardiac rehabilitation if it were prescribed.[43] Other studies have found that, in the mental health care setting, lower-class patients are "diagnosed as aberrant more frequently than middle-class patients."[44]

Women, too, are often held in low regard by health care professionals. One study found, for example, that physicians "like" male patients more than they like female patients.[45] ("Liking" was defined to include "warmth, respect, interest, and enthusiasm for seeing" the patient.) In another study, the vast majority of physicians referred to a woman when they were asked to describe "the typical complaining patient," while yet another study found that doctors applied the label "crock" (meaning a patient who is likely to give unreliable information) more often to women than to men. Studies also have found that "physicians believe women to be more mentally disturbed, to have more social problems and other vague symptoms, and to be less stoic than men during illness."[46]

The clinical context is ripe for the influence of such biases on decision making. The inherent uncertainty of diagnosis and treatment decisions, the ambiguity of patient symptoms and behavior,[47] and the wide discretion accorded medical professionals all create a situation in which "provider (and patient) presuppositions, attitudes, and fears that engender racial disparities have wide space to operate."[48] In other words, medical decision making takes place in a setting that is inherently uncertain and ambiguous. As does normative ambiguity generally, such "clinical uncertainty creates a portal for the entry" of "stereotypes and biases, conscious or unconscious, [to] shape the exercise of discretion in systematic fashion and [to] result in disparities."[49]

The standard practice of noting a patient's race as part of her case exacerbates these tendencies not only by transmitting the idea that race is a relevant factor but also by activating automatic stereotyping processes. Once those stereotypes are activated, it is difficult for the doctor to avoid applying them because the "cognitive busyness" inherent in medical decision making promotes their application.[50] Additional constraints built into the situation—time pressure, resource limitations, lack of complete and accurate information, heavy clinical loads, lack of a preexisting relationship between doctor and patient, rotating staffs, and physical stresses such as sleeplessness—also promote the use of "mental shortcuts" such as racial stereotypes and profiles and, accordingly, increase the probability that physicians will interpret patients' symptoms or prescribe treatment plans differentially based on race.[51]

As the Institute of Medicine explained in its 2002 report, given the situational constraints under which they function,

> [d]octors must depend on inferences about severity based on what they can see about the illness and on what else they observe about the patient (e.g., race). The exact same symptom information can lead the physician to make different clinical decisions depending on the other characteristics of the patient. Physicians can therefore be viewed as operating with prior beliefs about the likelihood of their patients' conditions, "priors" that will be different according to age, gender, SES [socioeconomic status], and possibly race/ethnicity. These priors—which are taught as a cognitive heuristic to medical students—as well as the information gained in a clinical encounter both influence medical decisions.[52]

Behavioral Confirmation in the Clinical Encounter: Medical Treatment as a Social Act

Even the clinical encounter, which might seem to present an opportunity to check the influence of race-based assumptions by allowing the patient to provide individualized information, may actually exacerbate rather than reduce the use of racial stereotypes. The doctor-patient relationship can be an important determinant of the quality of care a patient receives, for the diagnosis and treatment of disease are not just technical processes but also social acts.[53] Studies have shown that the quality of interaction between doctor and patient can have a significant effect on patients' health. In particular, higher quality care and better medical outcomes have been associated with a more "participatory," teamlike style of medical decision making involving give-and-take between doctor and patient. In that ideal relationship, the doctor involves the patient in treatment decisions by "providing treatment options, a sense of control over treatment decisions, and a sense of responsibility for care."[54]

Whether this relationship is achieved depends in large part on the doctor's perceptions of and feelings toward the patient. Generally, physicians' perceptions of patients' "likability" and competence have been found to influence their treatment of patients. For example, physicians tend to give less time, attention, and follow-up care to those whom they consider deviant or less likable.[55] In addition, doctors give less information to, seek less information from, and are less likely to attend to information offered by patients whom they regard as less intelligent or rational.[56] Furthermore, the same kinds of "immediate" behaviors that have been found to produce more positive performances in job interviews—sitting at the patient's level, maintaining eye contact, having a relaxed posture, nodding, and making encouraging sounds—also correlate with a better quality of health care.[57] Experts regard these and similar behaviors as positive aspects of physician nonverbal behavior.[58] In fact, these nonverbal behaviors may be both more important indicators of a doctor's regard for the patient and harder to fake than verbal friendliness.[59] When a physician feels uncomfortable with or dislikes a patient, not only is she less likely to behave in that immediate, patient-centered fashion but she may even cut off the encounter prematurely, before a thorough interview or examination can be completed.

Moreover, patients' satisfaction with their medical care affects their medical outcomes and is positively related to how much their doctors like them.[60] As in other social interactions, patient satisfaction and physician liking appear to have a "mutually reinforcing effect" within the medical encounter, as the patient and doctor send and respond to cues that increase their liking for one another. Likewise, feelings of discomfort or distrust between patient and doctor can be reciprocated and reinforced through interaction. For example, patients who feel that their doctors do not respect or are not interested in them may react by providing the doctor with less information about their symptoms or asking fewer questions about their conditions. Such behavior in turn may reinforce the doctor's perception that the patient is not intelligent or rational and discourage the doctor from asking questions of or sharing information with the patient. Similarly, a patient who does not trust or feel an affiliation with his doctor may be less inclined to comply with a prescribed treatment plan.[61]

While these studies suggest the operation of a self-fulfilling prophecy in doctor-patient relationships generally, there is good reason to believe that behavioral confirmation of prior expectations is especially problematic in *interracial* clinical encounters. It bears emphasizing that most encounters between patients of color and their physicians *will* be interracial, for the medical profession historically has failed to achieve a proportionate representation of racial and ethnic minorities and continues to fall short in this regard.[62] Greater racial and ethnic diversity among health care providers that reflects the diversity of the patient population could promote stronger doctor-patient relationships and reduce the influence of stereotypes within clinical encounters for, as the Institute of Medicine report observed, "[r]acial concordance of patient and provider is associated with greater patient participation in care processes, higher patient satisfaction, and greater adherence to treatment."[63]

A number of factors—the kinds of stereotypes and suspicions doctors hold of minority patients, patients' stereotypes of doctors, the structure and constraints of the interaction, and the institutional setting in which it occurs—can all converge in an encounter that convinces both doctor and patient of the accuracy of their negative expectations and results in the provision of inadequate care. Recent studies based on patient reports and third-party observations suggest a specific connection between doctors' negative views of racial minorities and a lower quality of interaction with patients from those groups. Rather than engaging them in the ideal, "participatory" or teamlike style of decision making that has been connected to greater patient satisfaction and better health outcomes, doctors tend to spend less time with, ask fewer questions of, and offer less information to such patients.[64] Moreover, because racial expectations can channel and constrain interaction in a confirmatory direction without providing evidence of their influence, the doctors' decisions or patients' choices that result can often be supported with neutral, nonracial justifications.[65]

Discomfort often leads people to turn to familiar scripts for their interaction. In examining his own struggle to overcome feelings of racial prejudice toward his minority patients, one doctor has described the relief with which he has resorted to "the well-practiced scripts that have become part of [his] standard doctoring repertoire"[66] at times when he has felt distracted or uncomfortable with a patient. Imposition of a script would tend to channel discussion in conformity with the doctor's preconceived notions and discourage the patient from offering individuating information. Doctors may also have greater difficulty communicating with patients from minority racial and ethnic groups, may interpret the "signals" they emit (such as reports of pain) differently from the signals emitted by White patients, and may make different decisions about diagnosis and treatment based on those signals despite having equal regard for each patient.[67] Implicit prejudice may show up in the doctor's nonverbal behavior as well, even if she does not recognize it.[68]

At the same time, patients of color may also hold negative expectations of White physicians: "These stereotypes may paint the physician as an arrogant clinician, or as 'the white man who experiments on minority patients,' or as a person who cannot be trusted to provide the whole truth."[69] Members of groups with a history or expectation of being treated poorly by medical professionals may place an especially high value on camaraderie with and respectful treatment by their doctors, and therefore may react especially negatively to physicians whose behavior suggests that they do not like, are not interested in, or do not respect them. In studies, African American patients have expressed a greater desire for camaraderie with their doctors than have White patients, but also (and unlike White patients) have expressed dissatisfaction with, mistrust of, and disdain for the health care system, based in part on their suspicions of racial and economic discrimination.[70] These suspicions can lead patients to misinterpret common medical practices as being intended to insult or degrade them. For example, African American patients may become offended when White health care professionals wear plastic gloves for a physical examination, believing that they do so because they are unwilling to touch a Black person's skin.[71] When a patient senses or suspects that the doctor feels unfavorably toward him or her, a "chain reaction" may be set off whereby the patient responds disagreeably or unhelpfully to the doctor's overtures—thereby maintaining the poor dynamic and "confirming" the physician's perception that the patient is not intelligent or rational and discouraging the doctor from asking questions of or sharing information with the patient.

Furthermore, just as situational constraints on medical decision making generally promote reflexive reference to racial profiles and stereotypes, so do the conditions of the typical medical interview promote the behavioral confirmation of such expectations. In addition to the time and resource limitations and cognitive "busyness" with which physicians generally must contend, the roles and respective goals of doctor and patient, the power differential between them, and common institutional practices and procedures help to create conditions that are almost ideal for the behavioral confirmation of erroneous expectations.

The roles designated for each party, coupled with the power differential that characterizes doctor-patient interactions, compound the effects of physicians' negative stereotypes by placing the doctor firmly in the position of the situation-defining "perceiver" and the patient in that of the responding "target." They take on these roles because the doctor must assess the patient and make judgments about the patient's condition and care. Therefore, as Whaley has pointed out, the doctor asks the questions that shape the interaction and, while the patient must respond to these questions, the doctor's own behavior is comparatively unconstrained.[72]

Power differences also promote both perceptual and behavioral confirmation of the doctor's stereotypes of the patient. The doctor-patient relationship is inherently one of unequal power and status for the simple reason that the doctor is the party with the expertise and authority in the interaction, while the patient occupies a vulnerable position by virtue of coming to the doctor in a less knowledgeable, help-seeking posture. Because "[o]ne person's ignorance is often the basis of another's power," this "competence gap" between doctor and patients helps to support the doctor's institutionalized privilege and maintain the "basic asymmetry in the doctor-patient relationship."[73] Aggravating this knowledge differential is the tendency of physicians to believe that patients "are unable to make [medical] decisions in a knowing, competent manner."[74] This sentiment has been traced to the Hippocratic Corpus, which states: "lacking professional training the client is too ignorant to be able to comprehend what information he gets and . . . he is, in any case, too upset at being ill to be able to use the information he does get in a manner that is rational and responsible."[75] Doctors also have the ability to enlarge their power by limiting the information they disclose to the patient or by controlling the patient's access to other medical resources. Moreover, the patient who is sick is almost by definition cast in the role of a social deviant.[76] As with other kinds of deviance or stigma, the patient's illness is another basis on which she may be accorded less respect and a lower status than the doctor.[77]

Specific medical situations may aggravate the power differential. One writer has vividly described how the gynecological examination—"an almost archetypal occasion for the expression of sex-stereotypic behavior"—may incorporate dynamics that compound the status and power differences inherent in the structure of the patient-doctor interaction:

> Power differences exist between the individuals not only because the physician is likely to be a man, but also because he is a high-status person with an advanced education and plentiful income. The woman comes seeking help or information from an acknowledged expert who is familiar with both the jargon and the routine. Further, during the examination she will be undressed, touched, and required to assume what is considered by many to be a humiliating posture. If, in addition, she is referred to as "honey" while he is addressed by surname and title, the power difference may be increased.[78]

Institutional norms and practices cement the status and power differential by establishing the organizationally appropriate behavior for the respective roles of patient and professional. Medical institutions structure activities and program people to accept their roles, thereby enhancing the divide between patients and staff. For example, the patient's "freedom of action and decision" are blocked through institutionally legitimate "means of social control," including the staff's discretion to dispense or deny privileges to or withhold information from patients while legitimizing their decisions to do so by framing them as "medical decisions."[79]

In addition, by defining a "good" patient as one who "is cooperative and makes few requests of the staff" and a "bad" patient as the opposite, the institution subtly "maintain[s] social distance between the patient and staff."[80] Even routine procedures to which a patient is subjected—being assigned and identified by a number rather than his name, providing information that "become[s] part of a quasi-public patient record," submitting to examinations, being "prevented from performing simple body functions without the assistance of others"—diminish the patient's sense of self and lower his status to make it compatible with the institution's interests.[81]

Furthermore, the power differential is often mutually accepted: several studies have found that health care professionals and patients alike "view the ideal patient as a cooperative, acquiescent person who plays an essentially deferential role."[82]

The goals of the typical medical encounter, combined with the constraints under which they must be met, encourage the individual practitioner to structure interactions in ways that play into the power differential to further promote behavioral confirmation of the doctor's expectations. A doctor's functions in a medical interview are similar to those of other professionals whose goals tend to promote the behavioral confirmation process. Like therapists and counselors, employers, and teachers, doctors must assess their interaction partners in an attempt to get a "predictable view" of them, so they can evaluate "their prognosis for improvement in treatment."[83] Given the time pressures under which they operate, the ambiguity and complexity of their tasks, and the amount of information they need to manage, doctors would be expected to adopt approaches to clinical encounters that both exacerbate the effects of the power differential and increase their reliance on stereotypes. A doctor who is called on to make a quick judgment after only a brief encounter with a patient may be motivated to structure the interaction and to process the information derived from it so as to confirm his or her preformed judgments, rather than to form an accurate impression. The goal of forming a quick impression has been found to cause perceivers to ask leading rather than open-ended questions, to focus on expectation-consistent information, and to interpret ambiguous information as confirming expectations.

The combination of situational pressures and negative expectations can affect not just the quality of the parties' relationship but also the accuracy of diagnosis. It may also lead doctors unwittingly to prescribe, and patients to prefer, treatment choices that are less than optimal.

Mental health diagnosis and treatment of African American patients provide an especially vivid illustration of the influence of racial bias, because the kinds of judgments that must be made can implicate a wide range of racial stereotypes (including the stereotypes of Blacks as being aggressive or violent, less complex intellectually or psychologically, or more likely to engage in substance abuse than Whites) and because mental health professionals may feel less empathy or optimism for Black patients than for White patients.[84] These stereotypes and attitudes may set off a self-fulfilling process by which a White mental health professional, feeling uncomfortable with a Black patient and expecting him to be aggressive or hostile, behaves in a racially prejudiced manner, leading the patient to act in conformity with such stereotypes and the clinician to make a more severe diagnosis or to recommend a more restrictive intervention than might actually be warranted. Further, White clinicians who do not appreciate their African American patients' mistrust of Whites may misinterpret their symptoms of "cultural paranoia" and misdiagnose their conditions—for example, mistaking depression for schizophrenia.[85] Similarly, a lack of familiarity with cultural factors may lead White mental health professionals to assess Asian American patients inappropriately.[86]

Doctors also might encourage patients to make treatment choices that are not ideally tailored to their situations but instead are consistent with the doctor's race-based assumptions. The inferiority of the decision might not be apparent, because the patient might seem to prefer that course over a better-suited treatment plan. To view that choice as solely based on "patient preference," however, can be misleading, because physicians have great power to shape patient preferences through their ability to control the way options are presented, as well as how much information is disclosed, and because patients are unlikely to go against a doctor's advice due to the physician's greater knowledge and power.[87]

Finally, a doctor's expectation that the patient will not comply with a demanding treatment regimen may produce its own confirmation, because the doctor may present the recommendation in a perfunctory or unassertive way or may convey negative expectations that "dampen" the patient's interest in and compliance with the recommended care. In addition, a patient who does not trust or feel an affiliation with his or her doctor may be less inclined to comply with a prescribed treatment plan,[88] and a patient who does not expect to benefit from medical care might rationally decide not to comply with the plan.[89]

When these factors culminate in inferior outcomes for patients of color, the reaction is not likely to be one of surprise. Racially disparate health outcomes have come to seem normal, even inevitable, and it may be hard to imagine an alternative state of affairs. The expectation that race is relevant is confirmed and reinforced when the predicted outcomes materialize but doctors fail to see the role that their race-related expectations played in producing their own supposed confirmation. The belief that race is relevant is perpetuated when statistics showing racially disparate medical outcomes provide "objective," empirical evidence of that fact. As a result of these failures of imagination, institutional bias in medicine becomes "an unseen, self-sustaining force."[90]

The Inadequacy of Individual Adjudication to Identify Biased Medical Care

Racially biased medical treatment is predictable, but we cannot predict exactly *when* it will occur and "[w]e might not even be able to identify when [it] *has* occurred."[91] Determining whether race was the "real" reason for a medical decision may be even more daunting a task than determining the real reason a candidate was not hired or a motorist was pulled over. As a result, individual adjudication under the currently dominant legal model is simply not suited to addressing the most common reasons for racially biased medical decision making. Under the federal laws that potentially create a private cause of action for racial discrimination in medical care, such as the equal protection clause and Title VI of the Civil Rights Act of 1964,[92] the plaintiff is required to prove that the defendant intended to discriminate.[93] The intentional discrimination model would not apply in most cases, however, because medical decision makers are, by and large, unlikely to be motivated by an explicit desire to deliver inferior care to patients of color. Furthermore, as the preceding discussion has shown, medical decision making is inherently complex and uncertain, and institutional, cognitive, and social influences interact with that ambiguity to simultaneously promote, obscure, and legitimize racially disparate medical treatment.

Racial bias therefore can infect diagnosis and treatment decisions not only without the decision maker's intending to discriminate on the basis of race but also without leaving evidence that it has affected the care delivered. Thus, in addition to being unable to prove that the defendant discriminated intentionally, the plaintiff may be unable to prove another essential element: "that discrimination in fact occurred—that he received different medical treatment because of his race . . . and not for some other reason."[94] As one legal scholar points out, "Health care providers making individualized medical decisions . . . can always offer a medical justification for their decision, even if the decision in fact arose from a conscious or unconscious reaction to the patient's race."[95] In deference to medical professionals' expertise and the complexity of their tasks, moreover, courts are reluctant to second-guess the nondiscriminatory reasons defendants offer for their decisions.[96] Furthermore, to the extent that a defendant followed standard medical practices, her treatment of the patient is unlikely to be seen as deficient, and those practices will continue to enjoy the assumption of legitimacy.

6

Overriding the Default

> The initial definition of the situation which has set the circle in motion must be abandoned. Only when the original assumption is questioned and a new definition of the situation introduced, does the consequent flow of events give lie to the assumption. Only then does the belief no longer father the reality.[1]

As we have seen, discrimination is locked in as the de facto standard, because it can occur without our awareness and because we regard discriminatory outcomes as normal. Discrimination can occur *by* default, because discrimination *is* the default.

How can we override the default?

Overriding the Default at Trial

This book began with the premise that legal prohibitions against discrimination are inadequate to redress the largest share of modern discrimination, particularly under the dominant model of intentional discrimination. The ensuing chapters have shown some of the reasons why: because the situations and processes that tend to promote discrimination also tend to mask it, many cases of disparate treatment never make it into the legal system. When a case does come to court, the discrimination in question might not meet the prevailing standard because the perpetrator might not have intended to discriminate or the challenged decision might appear to be justified on nondiscriminatory grounds. To the extent that legal standards institutionalize a preference for the normal, behavior that accords with custom or standard practice may be insulated from liability. Significant improvement, therefore, cannot depend on individual adjudication, but instead requires structural, institutional, and social change.

While the book's central message is indeed the inadequacy of legal determinations to right discriminatory wrongs, the lessons we have learned also suggest some possibilities for marginal improvements in legal decision making that *itself* might incorporate discrimination by default. That is, among the lessons that social psychology has taught us are the ways in which situational racism, self-fulfilling stereotypes, and failures of imagination creep into legal decision making and reinforce the effects of unconscious bias in the larger world. As we have seen, situational racism can come into play when jurors are not mindful of the need to guard against, and therefore act on, racial bias. Self-fulfilling stereotypes might taint a jury's verdict when the judge covertly communicates to jurors her expectation that a defendant is guilty. And failures of imagination can cause juries to absolve the perpetrator and blame the victim of discrimination when they can easily imagine the victim, but not the perpetrator, behaving differently.

Each of these default processes might be checked through measures that lawyers or judges can take. To combat situational racism, a lawyer might increase the normative clarity of the decision before the jury. To counteract any biases she might have communicated to the jury, the judge might simplify the questions she presents them. To overcome failures of imagination, an attorney might construct counterfactual narratives that focus on the perpetrator or the outcome.

Increasing normative clarity can help jurors to "resist falling into the discrimination habit."[2] Jody Armour has proposed a controversial but persuasive idea to help lawyers combat unconscious bias when it might taint jurors' decisions: the lawyer should purposefully and explicitly *inject* race into the case. But Armour's proposal is far more sophisticated and virtuous than a simple call to "play the race card." He does not recommend making reference to race in every case, and he proposes that racial references be used only if they are carefully timed and crafted to enhance, and not subvert, the rationality of jurors' decision making.

Thus, Armour flatly opposes covert appeals to racial fears and stereotypes, such as a prosecutor might employ in urging jurors to convict a Black defendant, or that a defense lawyer might use—as did the defense in the famous subway vigilante case, *People v. Bernhard Goetz*—to justify his White client's shooting a Black victim as self-defense. Instead, Armour proposes that jurors who may have been exposed to cues that trigger unconscious stereotypes, including the aforementioned rationality-subverting racial appeals, be challenged "to reexamine and resist their discriminatory responses" to "enhance the rationality of the fact-finding process."[3] Reminding jurors of their egalitarian beliefs during *voir dire* or opening statements, for example, can lead them to check and control the unconscious, automatic processes that can undermine rational evaluation of the evidence by channeling jurors' decisions in a discriminatory direction.[4]

Likewise, greater clarity can decrease the potential for a judge to influence the jury by unwittingly transmitting her biased expectations of a party. Recall that studies have found that judges may, through their nonverbal behavior, "leak" to jurors their expectations that a defendant will be found guilty. Jurors might pick up on these cues and evaluate the defendant in accordance with the judge's expectations.[5] A follow-up to those covert communication studies found that simplifying jury instructions can reduce the influence of judges' expectations on jurors' decisions. That is, if jurors receive clear, plainly worded instructions instead of the complex, often confusing, standard jury instructions commonly drafted by judicial or bar groups, they understand the relevant points of law, and hence their job, more clearly and are less likely to look to the judge for clues to the proper verdict.[6] Once again, situational clarity can counteract the effects of biased expectations.

To counteract another discriminatory default, plaintiffs' attorneys can take a page from the defense lawyers' book and make more effective use of counterfactual arguments. Defense lawyers commonly use two complementary strategies to reduce their clients' responsibility: one is to paint the defendant's behavior as utterly normal and conventional, and hence as unchangeable and less causal. Another is to focus on what the plaintiff might have done differently to avoid the harm that befell her. These strategies exploit the general tendency of observers to seek explanations for negative outcomes in the behavior of victims, while overlooking the perpetrator's behavior as "background" information.

Plaintiffs' attorneys could turn these strategies on their heads by employing the converse approaches.[7] To combat defense attorneys' attacks on the victim's behavior—"If only she had said no," or its converse, "What if she had not fought back?" or the similar "What were those Black men doing in a White neighborhood?"—the plaintiff's attorney could turn the tables and point out that the perpetrator could have acted differently and produced a different, more positive outcome. To counter the popular perception that the perpetrator discriminated out of a deep-seated, irrational "distaste" for other races, or the similar assumption that men rape or sexually harass out of uncontrollable biological urges, the attorney can emphasize the calculating, power-enhancing motivations that underlie these behaviors. They can also underline the exceptionality of the perpetrator's behavior—noting, for example, that supervisors who make sexual overtures to employees violate expectations for their role.[8] Another way to make the perpetrator's conduct more mutable, and hence more causal, is to focus on actions he took that he easily could have avoided—pointing out, for example, that rather than go on the attack, the perpetrator could have let an unfamiliar person walk through his neighborhood unmolested.

Conversely, the attorney can counteract defense attempts to make the plaintiff's behavior appear causal by using "even if" narratives. That is, the victim's attorney can point out that even if the victim had acted differently, the outcome would have been the same. This kind of counterfactual is most useful in situations where the perpetrator intended to produce the negative outcome.

Recall the case of the synagogue bombing in France. As noted previously, the fact that Jews were the intended victims rendered their deaths less poignant than those of "innocent" passersby. However, it is also apparent that the perpetrator was the person in that case who had the most control over the outcome; if he had not targeted the synagogue, *no one* would have been hurt. Emphasizing the perpetrator's primary role in producing the outcome can counteract a blame-lowering argument that might paint the perpetrator's conduct as inevitable and shift the focus to what the victim could have done differently: even if the victims had acted otherwise, the perpetrator was the one who determined the result.[9]

Prescription for Change: Altering the Situation

Even with improved advocacy and procedures, individual adjudication will fall short. Overriding the discriminatory standard requires comprehensive changes to disrupt the default processes that promote discrimination. The first step, therefore, must be to recognize and overcome the discrimination-promoting preference for conventional or standard practices, so that we are receptive to the institutional changes that are most effective. Useful strategies could include increasing the normative clarity of otherwise ambiguous situations by making goals definite and clear—for example, by measuring outcomes in objective, aggregate terms. Another approach is to alter the conditions under which parties interact, both to increase normative clarity and to reduce pressures that promote the behavioral confirmation of expectations.

Proposals for reform in medical care offer a promising array of possibilities. Citing the inadequacy of individual adjudication under current legal standards to identify, redress, and eliminate racial disparities in medical care, legal experts have asserted that real reform will come, instead, through efforts that focus on altering the institutions and systems in which medical decisions are made and care is delivered.[10]

Consider, as an example of the power of institutional change to achieve results, the desegregation of American hospitals in the 1960s. Racial segregation of medical facilities and care was deeply entrenched in the United States from the days of slavery through the middle of the twentieth century. Efforts within the African American community, such as developing their own hospitals, medical and nursing schools, and having individual physicians obtain admitting privileges to White hospitals, brought some measure of improvement, but were not sufficient to address the basic deficiencies in care and stigmatization of Black patients that segregation entailed.[11]

An equal protection challenge in 1963, *Simkins v. Moses H. Cone Memorial Hospital*[12]—"health care's *Brown v. Board of Education*"[13]—was the first step in the surprisingly smooth desegregation of hospitals nationwide, an achievement that was realized in 1966. Desegregation "occurred quickly, quietly and voluntarily" following that decision, once Title VI of the 1964 Civil Rights Act and the Medicare and Medicaid programs of 1965 were adopted. The key to the accomplishment was not, however, Title VI's mere prohibition against racial discrimination, but the decision of President Lyndon B. Johnson to tie a hospital's receipt of Medicare funds (a "substantial infusion of federal dollars") to its signing "an assurance of Title VI compliance certifying that it did not discriminate or segregate on the basis of race, color, or national origin and that the facility was in compliance with Title VI guidelines." Although President Johnson was warned that his goal of obtaining Title VI compliance and implementing the Medicare program within one year was "seemingly impossible" and that his plan might backfire, "[t]he boldness paid off": within four months, "over [ninety-two] percent of American hospitals were integrated." And, in contrast to the slow and painful process of school desegregation, all this occurred "without massive resistance, public demonstrations or protests."[14]

Several factors came together to produce this quick and dramatic result:

> First, the financial incentives were clear, strong, and unambiguous. Federal Medicare dollars began flowing only after hospitals integrated and the federal agency certified compliance with Title VI guidelines. . . .
>
> Second, the . . . effort involved no blaming and no sanctioning. The effort was entirely forward looking. . . . No questions were asked about past behavior and no justifications were needed.
>
> Third, all hospitals were subject to the same financial pressure. . . . White patients would simply have to adapt because there were few, if any, segregated hospitals to which to flee.
>
> Fourth, the goal, dismantling overt segregation, was a visible one that was easily verifiable. . . . The goal was obvious. Hospitals understood what was expected of them. . . .[15]

In other words, the government's use of financial incentives promoted straightforward decisions to integrate while it eliminated factors that might reward or justify decisions to do otherwise. First, the government created a goal—eliminate racial segregation in order to get Medicare funds—that directed the hospitals' behavior in the desired direction, and it provided an objective and visible means of measuring a hospital's attainment of that goal. Second, by putting that goal in "clear, strong and unambiguous" terms, it eliminated the potential for ambiguity that might mask racial disparities. Third, it offered no "out" or attractive alternative to compliance because its incentives were appealing to all hospitals and no hospital stood to gain by remaining segregated in order "to accommodate white prejudice." Finally, the plan did not rely on determinations of individual "fault" and hence did not create the need—or, more important, provide the opportunity—for past decisions with racially disparate impact to be justified on some purportedly legitimate ground.[16]

The story of hospital desegregation through Medicare funding incentives is, at its most obvious, a story of incentives at the institutional level altering behavior at the institutional level. Perhaps less obvious is the potential for change at the highest level to motivate and channel change at lower levels—even at the levels of the social and cognitive processes that, as we have seen, join with institutional processes to produce widespread racial disparities in medical care. Institutional reform has the potential to "channel *clinical discretion* in ways that reduce racial disparity."[17]

Institutional reform, in other words, can alter the direction of medical decision making by altering the situation in which medical decisions are made. Of course, these institutional changes should include examining, redressing, or eliminating practices that teach racially biased thinking and interaction. Important examples of such changes would include eliminating the "silent curriculum" by which racial myths are transmitted and reinforced, recruiting a more diverse group of medical professionals to serve the diverse population of patients, and interrogating the practice of racialized medical research.

Institutional reforms need not stop at those, however, for invisible situational factors could continue to channel medical decision making in a racially biased direction. To eliminate factors that promote and mask racial bias, therefore, institutions should follow the example of hospital desegregation by first creating the means to evaluate racial equality in medical treatment and outcomes in the aggregate, rather than on an individual basis where racial bias might escape notice or be explained away. Second, they should reduce the ambiguity of medical decision making and limit the potential for seemingly nondiscriminatory factors to provide justification for racially biased care. Finally, they should alter the goals, structure, and conditions of doctor-patient interactions in order to disrupt the potential for the behavioral confirmation of both parties' erroneous expectations of one another to influence their care and compliance.

A number of legal scholars have advocated the use of financial and other institutional incentives (whether positive incentives such as "bonuses" or negative ones like withholding funds) based on objective measures of racial equality in care—a proposal that mirrors the successful hospital desegregation initiative of the 1960s. They have proposed, for example, that federal funding, insurance payments, or hospital accreditation decisions be tied to an institution's delivery of racially equitable health care as measured by data on the use of services and choice of therapeutic alternatives or other performance criteria, "including patient satisfaction, rates of childhood immunization," and use of specified procedures.[18] These suggestions have the potential to both unmask racial disparity and channel racial equality in care because they measure racial disparities in the aggregate, making the disparities visible to both the institution and outside observers such as regulatory bodies, patients, and other medical institutions. The result of this openness should, according to its advocates, create internal incentives and peer pressure for the institution to rethink its policies and practices. Data collection would compel institutions to "think about race" and to begin an "internal dialogue" examining their assumptions and decisions,[19] creating a climate that "encourages education, change and improvement."[20]

Making racial equity a goal for the institution, and therefore a goal for individual professionals within the institution, should also affect the dynamics of doctor-patient interactions in a way that encourages doctors to seek individualized information from the patient and reduces the potential for behavioral confirmation of their stereotype-based expectations. As social psychologists have found, perceivers tend to pay more attention to individualized information about targets and to consider how external factors might be affecting their conduct in situations in which they are motivated to make accurate judgments (as opposed to confirming their predictions) and when they are aware that their decisions will be compared to objective criteria. Furthermore, monitoring patient satisfaction as well as clinical decisions and outcomes should have a positive effect on clinical encounters and reduce the potential for behavioral confirmation to the extent that it gives the patient greater power in the interaction and encourages the doctor to try to get along with the patient or to make the patient "like" him or her.

In addition to proposing that racial disparities be made more visible and the achievement of racial equity be rewarded, legal scholars have advocated altering the situation in which doctors interact with patients and make decisions. Their suggested reforms would channel those interactions and decisions to reduce racial disparity by limiting the ambiguity of medical decision making and reducing the situational constraints that promote racially biased decisions. Some propose, for example, that institutions reduce the opportunities for undetected bias to infect clinical decisions by limiting the amount of discretion afforded doctors in their treatment choices. They recognize that a balance must be struck between "the goal of reducing racial disparities and the virtues of greater clinical flexibility,"[21] but also point out that variations that are not based on scientific evidence are the kind most likely to produce unwarranted racial disparity.[22] Health plans could publish clinical practice protocols, "with supporting evidence and argument" that would be "open to professional and consumer review,"[23] and "professional medical societies, government bodies, or health care payers" might disseminate "clinical practice guidelines [that] . . . give individual practitioners the ability to practice evidence-based medicine."[24]

Institutions can also adopt measures to alter the conditions of the doctor-patient interaction through the use of "more nuanced" financial incentives than they currently employ. (One writer has noted that existing cost control measures already create financial incentives and disincentives, but they tend to "amplif[y] the social impact of . . . stereotypes and failures of empathy"[25] and therefore contribute to health care disparities.) These reforms could be directed at encouraging participatory decision making between doctor and patient, as well as at reducing the time pressures and cognitive load placed on doctors. For example, insurers could cover desirable practices, such as using language translation services or spending more time with patients and their families, or reward measures of patient satisfaction. In addition, government standards for Medicaid managed care plans could incorporate requirements for "the stability of patients' assignments to primary care providers (and these providers' accessibility), reasonable maximum patient loads per primary physician, and minimum time allotments for patient visits."[26] Reforms such as these have the potential to reduce the small, unnoticed situational factors that, in the aggregate, channel behavioral confirmation of, as well as the exercise of clinical discretion based on, racial stereotypes.

We cannot make substantial progress toward racial equity in medical care unless we "move from a backward looking focus on blame" and adopt multiple, creative approaches to change "old patterns of behavior."[27] The proposed reforms discussed above have the potential to challenge the "unseen, self-sustaining force"[28] of racial bias in medical care by disrupting the processes by which it operates. We must, as Merton wrote, "cut[] off their sustenance" through "deliberate institutional change."[29]

Accountability-Based Policing

Discrimination in other areas can be disrupted through similar measures.

Law enforcement agencies throughout the country have adopted a number of policies and strategies to reduce officers' reliance on racial profiling, whether intentional or reflexive. The ideal would be "to remove race from police decision making altogether" so that police "just focus on behavior"[30]—a challenge, to be sure. That ideal may be difficult to attain, but several strategies might lead us closer to a world in which race-based policing is more an aberration and less a standard practice.

The most effective reforms rest on the basic premise that change must come through public accountability and from the top of the organization. As might be expected, these strategies include communicating clear policies prohibiting the use of race as a basis for predicting criminality (as opposed to using race to identify a specific suspect based on a reliable physical description), training officers to help them understand how bias can creep into their decision making and to deal more effectively with different racial and ethnic groups with whom they may have contact, and data collection to get a complete and accurate picture of any problems that exist so they can be addressed.[31]

Other ideas aim to alter the situations in which and conditions under which officers work. First, some departments have adopted policies that specifically limit officers' discretion or channel it appropriately. For example, the law allows police to ask for consent to search a motor vehicle whether or not they have reason to suspect they will find evidence of a crime. Department policy need not grant officers the full scope of this discretion, however. A police department—or even the prosecutor, who controls which cases get to court—could limit consent searches to situations in which the officer can articulate a basis for reasonable suspicion. Likewise, requiring officers to write reports of all traffic stops explaining why they made the stop can prod them to "think twice" before making a stop.[32]

Altering the way in which officers and citizens interact *after* a stop can both help to improve race relations and prevent the self-fulfilling process by which tensions often escalate. Policies that emphasize the value of courteous, fair, and respectful treatment of citizens—perhaps providing a script of the information officers must give and reminding them to say "please" and "thank you" and to apologize for the inconvenience—can help to keep interracial encounters from "degenerat[ing] into a downward spiral of conflict, confrontation, and mutual contempt."[33]

Finally, changing incentive structures within police departments can also alter behavior for the good. Rather than reward officers on the basis of the number of traffic stops made, departments might give recognition to those officers who develop creative crime-prevention solutions in cooperation with the community.[34]

The multiple, symbiotic processes by which situations channel racism and stereotypes confirm themselves also serve to obscure and entrench the dynamics that produce disparate treatment and could justify our despair that society can ever break out of this "tragic, often vicious, circle."[35] But as Merton wrote in 1948, and as this book has argued, we can and we must thwart the self-fulfilling prophecy of discrimination by altering the situations in which—and disrupting the processes by which—it is realized.

Notes

Notes to Chapter 1

1. *Webster's Ninth New Collegiate Dictionary* 332 (1986).

2. See Barry Schwartz, *The Paradox of Choice: Why More Is Less* (2004).

3. Cf. Todd D. Rakoff, "Social Structure, Legal Structure, and Default Rules: A Comment," 3 *S. Cal. Interdisciplinary L. J.* 19, 27 (1994).

4. See Andrew J. McClurg, "A Thousand Words Are Worth a Picture: A Privacy Tort Response to Computer Data Profiling," 98 *Nw. U. L. Rev.* 63, 66, 74 n. 71, 82 (2003). For a detailed description of the process one Internet advertising company used to gather information, see In re DoubleClick Inc. Privacy Litigation, 154 F. Supp. 2d 497, 502–05 (S.D.N.Y. 2001).

5. Steve Krug, *Don't Make Me Think! A Common Sense Approach to Web Usability* (2000).

6. See McClurg, *supra*, at 94 n. 201.

7. *Id.*, at 94–95 n. 205.

8. See, e.g., Russell Korobkin, "Inertia and Preference in Contract Negotiation: The Psychological Power of Default Rules and Form Terms," 51 *Vand. L. Rev.* 1583 (1998).

9. Australian Broadcasting Corporation, "US Bans Time-Honoured Typeface," *ABC Online*, Jan. 30, 2004 (http://www.abc.net.au/news/newsitems/s1034726.htm). See also Lawrence Downes, "Retired Font Seeks New Opportunities," *N.Y. Times*, Feb. 8, 2004; Paul Shaw, "State Department Bans Courier New 12, except for Treaties," *AIGA Journal of Design and Typography*, March 10, 2004 (http://journal.aiga.org/content.cfm?ContentAlias=_getfullarticle&aid=340218).

10. Malcolm Gladwell, *Blink: The Power of Thinking without Thinking* 189–97, 242–44 (2005).

11. *Id.* at 194.

12. *Id.* at 242.

13. *Id.* at 194–96.

14. *Id.* at 197.

15. See *id.* at 232–33. See also Joshua Correll et al., "The Police Officer's Dilemma: Using Ethnicity to Disambiguate Potentially Threatening Individuals," 83 *J. Personality and Social Psychology* 1314 (2002); Anthony G. Greenwald, Mark A. Oakes, and Hunter G. Hoffman, "Targets of Discrimination: Effects of Race on Responses to Weapons Holders," 39 *J. Experimental Social Psychology* 399 (2003); B. Keith Payne, "Prejudice and Perception: The Role of Automatic and Controlled Processes in Misperceiving a Weapon," 81 *J. Personality and Social Psychology* 181 (2001).

16. See Ian F. Haney Lopéz, "Institutional Racism: Judicial Conduct and a New Theory of Racial Discrimination," 109 *Yale L.J.* 1717 (2000).

17. Brant T. Lee, "The Network Economic Effects of Whiteness," 53 *American U. L. Rev.* 1259, 1263–64 (2004) (citations omitted). See also Daria Roithmayr, "Barriers to Entry: A Market Lock-In Model of Discrimination," 86 *Va. L. Rev.* 727, 732–33 (2000).

18. Roithmayr, *supra*, at 732–34.

19. Lee, *supra*, at 1270.

20. Roithmayr, *supra*, at 735.

21. *Id.* at 754–61.

22. Richard Delgado, "Official Elitism or Institutional Self Interest? 10 Reasons Why UC-Davis Should Abandon the LSAT (and Why Other Good Law Schools Should Follow Suit)," 34 *UC-Davis L. Rev.* 593, 607 (2001).

23. *Id.* at 598.

24. See Richard O. Lempert et al., "Michigan's Minority Graduates in Practice: The River Runs through Law School," 25 *L. and Soc. Inquiry* 394, 459–61, 463–68 (2000). But see Delgado, *supra*, at 599–600; William C. Kidder, "Does the LSAT Mirror or Magnify Racial and Ethnic Differences in Educational Attainment? A Study of Equally Achieving 'Elite' College Students," 89 *Cal. L. Rev.* 1055, 1101–03 (2001).

25. See Delgado, *supra*, at 601; Kidder, "Does the LSAT Mirror or Magnify," *supra*, at 1104; Lempert et al., *supra*, at 461–62, 468–90, 497.

26. Delgado, *supra*, at 608. See also William C. Kidder, "The Rise of the Testocracy: An Essay on the LSAT, Conventional Wisdom, and the Dismantling of Diversity," 9 *Tex. J. Women and L.* 167, 200–04 (2000).

27. Delgado, *supra*, at 601–02.

28. See *id.* at 602–05. Cf. Kidder, "Does the LSAT Mirror or Magnify," *supra*, at 1094 (discussing studies that "suggest that the LSAT 'discriminates' against students of color by magnifying racial/ethnic differences compared to what occurs in college or law school").

29. Delgado, *supra*, at 605–06.

30. See Claude M. Steele, "A Threat in the Air: How Stereotypes Shape

Intellectual Identity and Performance," 52 *American Psychologist* 613 (1997).

31. Roithmayr, *supra*, at 762–63.

32. *Id.* at 736.

33. *Id.* at 767.

34. *Id.* at 775–85.

35. Lee, *supra*, at 1260.

36. Linda Hamilton Krieger, "The Content of Our Categories: A Cognitive Bias Approach to Discrimination and Equal Employment Opportunity," 47 *Stan. L. Rev.* 1161, 1217 (1995).

37. See, e.g., Martha Chamallas, "Deepening the Legal Understanding of Bias: On Devaluation and Biased Prototypes," 74 *S. Cal. L. Rev.* 747 (2001); Haney López, *supra*; Linda Hamilton Krieger, "Civil Rights Perestroika: Intergroup Relations after Affirmative Action," 86 *Cal. L. Rev.* 1251 (1998); Krieger, "The Content of Our Categories," *supra*; Charles R. Lawrence III, "The Id, the Ego, and Equal Protection: Reckoning with Unconscious Racism," 39 *Stan. L. Rev.* 317 (1987); Anthony C. Thompson, "Stopping the Usual Suspects: Race and the Fourth Amendment," 74 *N.Y.U. L. Rev.* 956 (1999).

38. Washington v. Davis, 426 U.S. 229, 237 (1976).

39. See Lawrence, *supra*, at 319.

40. See Chamallas, *supra*, at 748–49.

41. See Krieger, "The Content of Our Categories," *supra*, at 1163.

42. Whren v. United States, 517 U.S. 806, 813 (1996).

43. Terry v. Ohio, 392 U.S. 1 (1968).

44. 517 U.S. 806.

45. Thompson, *supra*, at 972.

46. *Id.*, quoting *Terry*, 392 U.S. at 14–15.

47. Thompson, *supra,* at 972, 982.

48. *Id.* at 981–82.

49. Krieger, "The Content of Our Categories," *supra*, at 1248.

50. See *id.* at 1168–69.

51. *Id.* at 1167.

52. *Id.*

53. *Id.*

54. Gary Blasi, "Advocacy against the Stereotype: Lessons from Cognitive Social Psychology," 49 *UCLA L. Rev.* 1241, 1242–46, 1266–72 (2002); Susan T. Fiske, "Examining the Role of Intent: Toward Understanding Its Role in Stereotyping and Prejudice," in *Unintended Thought* 253, 268–75 (James S. Uleman and John A. Bargh, eds., 1989); Krieger, "Civil Rights Perestroika," *supra*, at 1309–11.

55. Lawrence, *supra*, at 325. See also Thomas Ross, "Innocence and Affirmative Action," 43 *Vand. L. Rev.* 297, 312 (1990).

Notes to Chapter 2

1. Linda Hamilton Krieger, "Civil Rights Perestroika: Intergroup Relations after Affirmative Action," 86 *Cal. L. Rev.* 1251, 1310–11 (1998).

2. See *id.* at 1310.

3. See Lu-in Wang, "The Complexities of 'Hate,'" 60 *Ohio St. L. J.* 799, 823–24 (1999).

4. See David A. Harris, "The Stories, the Statistics, and the Law: Why 'Driving while Black' Matters," 84 *Minn. L. Rev.* 265, 294 (1999).

5. See Daniel T. Gilbert and Patrick S. Malone, "The Correspondence Bias," 117 *Psychol. Bull.* 21, 26 (1995).

6. Susan T. Fiske and Shelley E. Taylor, *Social Cognition* 68 (1991). See also Gilbert and Malone, *supra*, at 35; Lee Ross and Richard E. Nisbett, *The Person and the Situation: Perspectives of Social Psychology* 142 (1991).

7. See generally Fiske and Taylor, *supra*, at 67–72; Ross and Nisbett, *supra*, at 125–38.

8. Gilbert and Malone, *supra*, at 25–26; Ross and Nisbett, *supra*, at 128.

9. See Erica Goode, "The Gorge-Yourself Environment," *N.Y. Times*, July 22, 2003, at D1.

10. Ross and Nisbett, *supra*, at 10–11 and 47–48.

11. *Id.* at 10.

12. John M. Darley and C. Daniel Batson, "From Jerusalem to Jericho: A Study of Situational and Dispositional Variables in Helping Behavior," 27 *J. Personality and Soc. Psychol.* 100 (1973).

13. See Ross and Nisbett, *supra*, at 49.

14. John M. Darley and Bibb Latané, "Bystander Intervention in Emergencies: Diffusion of Responsibility," 8 *J. Personality and Soc. Psychol.* 377 (1968).

15. See Stanley Milgram, *Obedience to Authority: An Experimental View* (1974). These famous experiments have inspired much discussion and analysis since Milgram first reported them. See, e.g., *Obedience to Authority: Current Perspectives on the Milgram Paradigm* (Thomas Blass, ed., 2000).

16. Milgram, *supra*, at 30, 31.

17. *Id.* at 149.

18. *Id.*

19. *Id.* at 150.

20. *Id.* at 107.

21. The studies also highlighted the double standard that individuals apply in explaining their own actions. Displaying the divergent biases typical of individuals in explaining their own negative and positive behavior, subjects who had complied to the end in administering the most severe shocks tended to place responsibility for their actions with the experimenter or even the "stupid" learner—that is, they attributed it to the situation—while those who disobeyed tended to attribute their decisions to their own strong values and characters. *Id.* at 7–8, 10, 203–04.

22. *Id.* at 5–10, 175–89; Ross and Nisbett, *supra*, at 52–53. Cf. Richard Delgado, "Norms and Normal Science: Toward a Critique of Normativity in Legal Thought," 139 *U. Pa. L. Rev.* 933, 944–46 (1991).

23. Samuel R. Sommers and Phoebe C. Ellsworth, "White Juror Bias: An Investigation of Prejudice against Black Defendants in the American Courtroom," 7 *Psychol., Pub. Pol'y and L.* 201 (2001); Samuel R. Sommers and Phoebe C. Ellsworth, "Race in the Courtroom: Perceptions of Guilt and Dispositional Attributions," 26 *Personality and Soc. Psychol. Bull.* 1367 (2000).

24. Sommers and Ellsworth, "White Juror Bias," *supra*, at 220. See also Patricia G. Devine, "Stereotypes and Prejudice: Their Automatic and Controlled Components," 56 *J. Personality and Social Psychology* 5, 15–16 (1989).

25. See Samuel L. Gaertner and John F. Dovidio, "The Aversive Form of Racism," in *Prejudice, Discrimination, and Racism* 61, 67–68 (John F. Dovidio and Samuel L. Gaertner, eds. 1986).

26. See Samuel L. Gaertner, "Helping Behavior and Racial Discrimination among Liberals and Conservatives," 25 *J. Personality and Soc. Psychol.* 335 (1973); Lauren G. Wispé and Harold B. Freshley, "Race, Sex, and Sympathetic Helping Behavior: The Broken Bag Caper," 17 *J. Personality and Soc. Psychol.* 59 (1971). For a review of studies of race and helping behavior, see Faye Crosby et al., "Recent Unobtrusive Studies of Black and White Discrimination and Prejudice: A Literature Review," 87 *Psychol. Bull.* 546 (1980).

27. See Gordon Hodson, John F. Dovidio, and Samuel L. Gaertner, "Processes in Racial Discrimination: Differential Weighting of Conflicting Information," 28 *Personality and Social Psychology Bulletin* 460 (2002); John F. Dovidio and Samuel L. Gaertner, "Aversive Racism and Selection Decisions: 1989 and 1999," 11 *Psychological Science* 319 (2000).

28. David L. Frey and Samuel L. Gaertner, "Helping and the Avoidance of Inappropriate Interracial Behavior: A Strategy That Perpetuates a Nonprejudiced Self-Image," 50 *J. Personality and Soc. Psychol.* 1083 (1986). See also Krieger, "Civil Rights Perestroika," *supra*, at 1324.

29. Samuel L. Gaertner and John F. Dovidio, "The Subtlety of White Racism, Arousal, and Helping Behavior," 35 *J. Personality and Soc. Psychol.* 691 (1977).

30. Samuel L. Gaertner et al., "Race of Victim, Nonresponsive Bystanders, and Helping Behavior," 117 *J. Soc. Psychol.* 69 (1982).

31. See Dovidio and Gaertner, "Aversive Racism and Selection Decisions," *supra*; Hodson et al., *supra*.

32. John F. Dovidio et al., "Racial Attitudes and the Death Penalty," 27 *J. Applied Soc. Psychol.* 1468 (1997).

33. James D. Johnson et al., "Justice Is Still Not Colorblind: Differential Racial Effects of Exposure to Inadmissible Evidence," 21 *Personality and Soc. Psychol. Bull.* 893 (1995).

34. *Id.* at 896–97.

35. Gaertner and Dovidio, "The Aversive Form of Racism," *supra*, at 73.

36. Devine, *supra*, at 15.

37. This account is the theory of aversive racism that has been offered by social psychologists Samuel L. Gaertner and John F. Dovidio. See generally John F. Dovidio and Samuel L. Gaertner, "On the Nature of Contemporary Prejudice: The Causes, Consequences, and Challenges of Aversive Racism," in *Confronting Racism: The Problem and the Response* 3 (Jennifer L. Eberhardt and Susan T. Fiske, eds., 1998); Gaertner and Dovidio, "The Aversive Form of Racism," *supra*.

38. Devine, *supra*, at 16.

39. See generally Jody David Armour, *Negrophobia and Reasonable Racism: The Hidden Costs of Being Black in America* 126–39 (1997); Devine, *supra*, at 15–16.

40. See generally, e.g., Armour, *supra*, at 126–39; Devine, *supra*, at 15–16; Dovidio and Gaertner, "On the Nature of Contemporary Prejudice," *supra*, at 4–8.

41. See Krieger, "Civil Rights Perestroika," *supra*, at 1308.

42. *Id.* at 1327.

43. Linda Hamilton Krieger, "The Content of Our Categories: A Cognitive Bias Approach to Discrimination and Equal Employment Opportunity," 47 *Stan. L. Rev.* 1161, 1170 (1995).

44. *Id.* at 1179. See also *id.* at 1177–79, 1213.

45. See *id.* at 1183, 1213. See also 42 U.S.C. §§ 2000e-2(m) and 2000e-5(g)(2)(B) (2000).

46. Harris, *supra*, at 311.

47. Anthony C. Thompson, "Stopping the Usual Suspects: Race and the Fourth Amendment," 74 *N.Y.U. L. Rev.* 956, 982 (1999).

48. Whren v. United States, 517 U.S. 806, 812–13 (1996).

49. For discussion of the difficulty of establishing a denial of equal protection in this situation, see David Cole, *No Equal Justice: Race and Class in the American Criminal Justice System* 39–40 (1999); Angela J. Davis, "Race, Cops, and Traffic Stops," 51 *U. Miami L. Rev.* 425, 436–38 (1997).

50. Thompson, *supra*, at 983.

51. Cole, *supra*, at 53. See also Harris, *supra*, at 319; Katheryn K. Russell, *The Color of Crime: Racial Hoaxes, White Fear, Black Protectionism, Police Harassment, and Other Macroaggressions* 1–13 (1998).

52. Thompson, *supra*, at 987–91. See also Devon W. Carbado, "(E)Racing the Fourth Amendment," 100 *Mich. L. Rev.* 946, 1032 (2002).

Notes to Chapter 3

1. See Joshua Correll et al., "The Police Officer's Dilemma: Using Ethnicity to Disambiguate Potentially Threatening Individuals," 83 *J. Personality and Social Psychology* 1314 (2002); Malcolm Gladwell, *Blink: The Power of Thinking without Thinking* 189–244 (2005); Anthony G. Greenwald, Mark A. Oakes, and Hunter G. Hoffman, "Targets of Discrimination: Effects of Race on Responses to Weapons Holders," 39 *J. Experimental Social Psychology* 399 (2003); B. Keith Payne, "Prejudice and Perception: The Role of Automatic and Controlled Processes in Misperceiving a Weapon," 81 *J. Personality and Social Psychology* 181 (2001).

2. See Claudia Goldin and Cecilia Rouse, "Orchestrating Impartiality: The Impact of 'Blind' Auditions on Female Musicians," 90 *American Economic Review* 715 (2000). See also Gladwell, *supra*, at 245–54.

3. Robert K. Merton, "The Self-Fulfilling Prophecy," 8 *Antioch Review* 193, 196 (1948).

4. Paul Watzlawick, "Self-Fulfilling Prophecies," in *The Production of Reality: Essays and Readings on Social Interactions* 425 (Jodi O'Brien and Peter Kollock, eds., 2d ed. 1997).

5. Russell A. Jones, *Self-Fulfilling Prophecies: Social, Psychological, and Physiological Effects of Expectancies* 58 (1977).

6. Merton, *supra*, at 196.

7. Richard D. Ashmore, "Prejudice: Causes and Cures," in *Social Psychology* (B. Collins, ed., 1970), quoted in Jones, *supra*, at 58.

8. David A. Harris, "The Stories, the Statistics, and the Law: Why 'Driving while Black' Matters," 84 *Minn. L. Rev.* 265, 297 (1999).

9. Nevada Dep't of Human Resources v. Hibbs, 538 U.S. 721, 736 (2003).

10. Linda Hamilton Krieger, "Civil Rights Perestroika: Intergroup Relations after Affirmative Action," 86 *Cal. L. Rev.* 1251, 1326 (1998).

11. These studies are described in Joshua Aronson et al., "The Effect of Stereotype Threat on the Standardized Test Performance of College Students," in *Readings about the Social Animal* 403 (Elliot Aronson, ed., 8th ed. 1999). See also Claude M. Steele, "A Threat in the Air: How Stereotypes Shape Intellectual Identity and Performance," 52 *American Psychologist* 613 (1997).

12. Jean-Claude Croizet and Theresa Claire, "Extending the Concept of Stereotype Threat to Social Class: The Intellectual Underperformance of Students from Low Socioeconomic Backgrounds," 24 *Personality and Social Psychology Bulletin* 588 (1998).

13. Thomas M. Hess et al., "The Impact of Stereotype Threat on Age Differences in Memory Performance," 58B *Journal of Gerontology: Series B: Psychological Sciences and Social Sciences* 3 (2003).

14. Jeff Stone et al., "Stereotype Threat Effects on Black and White Athletic Performance," 77 *J. Personality and Social Psychology* 1213 (1999).

15. Aronson et al., *supra*, at 404.

16. Steele, *supra*, at 614.

17. Aronson et al., *supra*, at 413.

18. Gregory M. Walton and Geoffrey L. Cohen, "Stereotype Lift," 39 *J. Experimental Social Psychology* 456 (2003).

19. Merton, *supra*, at 195.

20. *Id.*

21. See Robert Rosenthal and Lenore Jacobson, *Pygmalion in the Classroom: Teacher Expectation and Pupils' Intellectual Development* (1968).

22. Robert Rosenthal, "Covert Communications in Laboratories, Classrooms, and the Truly Real World," 12 *Current Directions in Psychological Science* 151, 152 (2003).

23. See Albert S. King, "Self-Fulfilling Prophecies in Training the Hard-Core: Supervisors' Expectations and the Underprivileged Workers' Performance," 52 *Soc. Sci. Q.* 369 (1971). See also Dov Eden, *Pygmalion in Management: Productivity as a Self-Fulfilling Prophecy* (1990).

24. Peter D. Blanck, Robert Rosenthal, and L. H. Cordell, Note, "The Appearance of Justice: Judges' Verbal and Nonverbal Behavior in Criminal Jury Trials," 89 *Stan. L. Rev.* 89 (1985).

25. Allen J. Hart, "Naturally Occurring Expectation Effects," 68 *J. Personality and Soc. Psychol.* 109 (1995), discussing Blanck et al., *supra*.

26. See Doré Butler and Florence L. Geis, "Nonverbal Affect Responses to Male and Female Leaders: Implications for Leadership Evaluations," 58 *J. Personality and Social Psychology* 48 (1990).

27. *Id.* at Hart, *supra*. See also Robert Rosenthal, "Covert Communica-

tion in Classrooms, Clinics, Courtrooms, and Cubicles," *American Psychologist*, Nov. 2002, at 839.

28. Steven L. Neuberg, "Expectancy-Confirmation Processes in Stereotype Tinged Social Encounters: The Moderating Role of Social Goals," in 7 *The Psychology of Prejudice, The Ontario Symposium* 103, 104 (Mark P. Zanna and James M. Olson, eds., 1994).

29. See Mark Snyder and William B. Swann Jr., "Behavioral Confirmation in Social Interaction: From Social Perception to Social Reality," 14 *J. Experimental Soc. Psychol.* 148 (1978) (hostile); Mark Snyder and William B. Swann Jr., "Hypothesis-Testing Processes in Social Interaction," 36 *J. Personality and Soc. Psychol.* 1202 (1978) (extroverted); Dana Christensen and Robert Rosenthal, "Gender and Nonverbal Decoding Skill as Determinants of Interpersonal Expectancy Effects," 42 *J. Personality and Soc. Psychol.* 75 (1982) (sociable); Saul M. Kassin et al., "Behavioral Confirmation in the Interrogation Room: On the Dangers of Presuming Guilt," 27 *L. and Human Behavior* 187 (2003) (guilty of a crime).

30. See, e.g., Dylan M. Smith et al., "Target Complicity in the Confirmation and Disconfirmation of Erroneous Perceiver Expectations: Immediate and Longer Term Implications," 73 *J. Personality and Soc. Psychol.* 974 (1997); Snyder and Swann, "Behavioral Confirmation in Social Interaction," *supra*, at 151, 156–57.

31. See Mark Snyder and Julie A. Haugen, "Why Does Behavioral Confirmation Occur? A Functional Perspective on the Role of the Target," 21 *Personality and Soc. Psychol. Bull.* 963 (1995).

32. Gladwell, *supra*, at 72–75.

33. Mark Snyder et al., "Social Perception and Interpersonal Behavior: On the Self-Fulfilling Nature of Social Stereotypes," 35 *J. Personality & Soc. Psychol.* 656 (1977). See also Mark Snyder, "When Belief Creates Reality: The Self-Fulfilling Impact of First Impressions," in *The Production of Reality*, *supra*, at 438.

34. Snyder et al., *supra*, at 662.

35. Snyder, *supra*, at 440.

36. Snyder et al., *supra*, at 661.

37. *Id.* at 663.

38. *Id.* (emphasis added).

39. *Id.* at 664.

40. Carl O. Word et al., "The Nonverbal Mediation of Self-Fulfilling Prophecies in Interracial Interaction," 10 *J. Experimental Soc. Psychol.* 109 (1974).

41. *Id.* at 110 (citing A. Mehrabian, "Inference of Attitudes from the

Posture, Orientation, and Distance of a Communicator," 32 *J. Consulting and Clinical Psychol.* 296 (1968)).

42. Word et al., *supra*, at 119.

43. See, e.g., Mark Chen and John A. Bargh, "Nonconscious Behavioral Confirmation Processes: The Self-Fulfilling Consequences of Automatic Stereotype Activation," 33 *J. Experimental Soc. Psychol.* 541 (1997); Berna J. Skrypnek and Mark Snyder, "On the Self-Perpetuating Nature of Stereotypes about Women and Men," 18 *J. Experimental Soc. Psychol.* 277 (1982); Carl L. von Bayer et al., "Impression Management in the Job Interview: When the Female Applicant Meets the Male (Chauvinist) Interviewer," 7 *Personality and Soc. Psychol. Bull.* 45 (1981); Mark P. Zanna and Susan J. Pack, "On the Self-Fulfilling Nature of Apparent Sex Differences in Behavior," 11 *J. Experimental Soc. Psychol.* 583 (1975).

44. See Chen and Bargh, *supra*.

45. This discussion draws from several articles that examine factors that promote and hinder behavioral confirmation. See generally John T. Copeland, "Prophecies of Power: Motivational Implications of Social Power for Behavioral Confirmation," 67 *J. Personality and Soc. Psychol.* 264 (1994); James L. Hilton and John M. Darley, "Constructing Other Persons: A Limit on the Effect," 21 *J. Exper. Soc. Psychol.* 1 (1985); Dale T. Miller and William Turnbull, "Expectancies and Interpersonal Processes," 37 *Ann. Rev. Psychol.* 233, 234 (1986); Steven L. Neuberg and Susan T. Fiske, "Motivational Influences on Impression Formation: Outcome Dependency, Accuracy-Driven Attention, and Individuating Processes," 53 *J. Personality and Soc. Psychol.* 431, 431–38 (1987); Steven L. Neuberg, "The Goal of Forming Accurate Impressions during Social Interaction: Attenuating the Impact of Negative Expectancies," 56 *J. Personality and Soc. Psychol.* 374 (1989); Mark Snyder, "Motivational Foundations of Behavioral Confirmation," 25 *Advances in Experimental Soc. Psychol.* 67, 79 (1992); Snyder and Haugen, "Role of the Target," *supra*; Mark Snyder and Julie A. Haugen, "Why Does Behavioral Confirmation Occur? A Functional Perspective on the Role of the Perceiver," 30 *J. Experimental Soc. Psychol.* 218 (1994); Mark Snyder and Arthur A. Stukas Jr., "Interpersonal Processes: The Interplay of Cognitive, Motivational, and Behavioral Activities in Social Interaction," 50 *Ann. Rev. Psychol.* 273 (1999); William B. Swann Jr. and Robin J. Ely, "A Battle of Wills: Self-Verification versus Behavioral Confirmation," 46 *J. Personality and Soc. Psychol.* 1287, 1299 (1984); Philip E. Tetlock and Jae Il Kim, "Accountability and Judgment Processes in a Personality Prediction Task," 52 *J. Personality and Soc. Psychol.* 700 (1987).

46. Miller and Turnbull, *supra*, at 234.

47. Snyder and Stukas, *supra*, at 283 (citing Steven L. Neuberg et al.,

"Perceiver Self-Presentation Goals as Moderators of Expectancy Influences: Ingratiation and the Disconfirmation of Negative Expectancies," 64 *J. Personality and Soc. Psychol.* 409 (1993)).

48. See Cynthia M. Frantz et al., "A Threat in the Computer: The Race Implicit Association Test as a Stereotype Threat Experience," 30 *Personality and Soc. Psychol. Bulletin* 1611 (2004).

49. J. Nicole Shelton, "Interpersonal Concerns in Social Encounters between Majority and Minority Group Members," 6 *Group Processes and Intergroup Relations* 171 (2003).

50. Snyder and Stukas, *supra*, at 287.

51. Snyder and Haugen, "The Role of the Perceiver," *supra*, at 241.

52. *Id.*

53. Edward E. Jones, "Interpreting Interpersonal Behavior: The Effects of Expectancies," 234 *Science* 41, 45 (1986).

54. von Baeyer et al., *supra*. See also Zanna and Pack, *supra*.

55. See Hai-Sook Kim and Robert S. Baron, "Exercise and the Illusory Correlation: Does Arousal Heighten Stereotypic Processing?" 24 *J. Experimental Soc. Psychol.* 366 (1988); Snyder and Stukas, *supra*, at 280.

56. Neuberg, "Expectancy-Confirmation Processes," *supra*, at 121 (citing Galen V. Bodenhausen, "Stereotypes as Judgmental Heuristics: Evidence of Circadian Variations in Discrimination," 1 *Psychol. Science* 319 (1990)) (emphasis in Neuberg).

57. See generally Cynthia Lee, *Murder and the Reasonable Man: Passion and Fear in the Criminal Courtroom* 87–88, 137–74 (2003); Katheryn K. Russell, *The Color of Crime: Racial Hoaxes, White Fear, Black Protectionism, Police Harassment, and Other Macroaggressions* 1–13 (1998); Lu-in Wang, "'Suitable Targets'? Parallels and Connections between 'Hate' Crimes and 'Driving while Black,'" 6 *Mich. J. Race and L.* 209, 227 (2001).

58. Regina Austin, "'A Nation of Thieves': Securing Black People's Right to Shop and Sell in White America," 119 *Utah L. Rev.* 147, 154 (1994).

59. See generally Deseriee A. Kennedy, "Consumer Discrimination: The Limitations of Federal Civil Rights Protection," 66 *Mo. L. Rev.* 275, 323 (2001); Jennifer Lee, "The Salience of Race in Everyday Life: Black Customers' Shopping Experiences in Black and White Neighborhoods," 27 *Work and Occupations* 353, 366–69 (2000).

60. Ronald Weitzer, "Racialized Policing: Residents' Perceptions in Three Neighborhoods," 34 *Law and Society Rev.* 129, 138 (2000).

61. This discussion of criminal interrogations draws from the "Bible" on interrogation methods, Fred E. Inbau, John E. Reid, Joseph P. Buckley, and Brian C. Jayne, *Criminal Interrogation and Confessions* (4th ed. 2001), and scholarly commentary on the techniques prescribed in that manual. See gen-

erally Kassin et al., *supra*; Richard A. Leo and Richard J. Ofshe, "The Consequences of False Confessions: Deprivations of Liberty and Miscarriages of Justice in the Age of Psychological Interrogation," 88 *J. Crim. L. and Criminology* 429 (1998); Richard J. Ofshe and Richard A. Leo, "The Social Psychology of Police Interrogation: The Theory and Classification of True and False Confessions," 16 *Studies in L., Politics and Soc'y* 189, 193 (1997); Welsh S. White, Miranda*'s Waning Protections: Police Interrogation Practices after* Dickerson 25 (2001); Welsh S. White, "*Miranda*'s Failure to Restrain Pernicious Interrogation Practices," 99 *Mich. L. Rev.* 1211, 1229 (2001); Welsh S. White, "False Confessions and the Constitution: Safeguards against Untrustworthy Confessions," 32 *Harv. C.R.-C.L. L. Rev.* 105, 108 and 108–09 n. 26 (1997).

62. A false confession is particularly harmful because confessions are considered to be the most persuasive evidence of a suspect's guilt. See, e.g., Leo and Ofshe, *supra*, at 429 (stating that "a confession is universally treated as damning and compelling evidence of guilt[.] . . . A false confession is therefore an exceptionally dangerous piece of evidence to put before anyone adjudicating a case."). Confession evidence is particularly powerful because the confessor is assumed to have firsthand knowledge of the event in question and "people find it difficult to believe that anyone would confess to a crime that he or she did not commit." Saul M. Kassin and Katherine Neumann, "On the Power of Confession Evidence: An Experimental Test of the Fundamental Difference Hypothesis," 21 *L. and Human Behav.* 469, 482 (1997).

63. Kassin et al., *supra*, at 189.

64. Ofshe and Leo, *supra*, at 193.

65. Kassin et al., *supra*, at 188–89 and 199. See also Christian A. Meissner and Saul M. Kassin, "'He's Guilty!': Investigator Bias in Judgments of Truth and Deception," 26 *L. and Human Behavior* 469 (2002).

66. White, Miranda*'s Waning Protections*, *supra*, at 27 (citing Fred Inbau, John E. Reid, and Joseph P. Buckley, *Criminal Interrogation and Confessions* 81–82 (1962) (earlier edition of the Inbau Manual)).

67. White, Miranda*'s Waning Protections*, *supra*, at 28–29.

68. *Id.* at 27.

69. Ofshe and Leo, *supra*, at 204–05.

70. *Id.* at 207.

71. *Id.* at 194.

72. See White, Miranda*'s Waning Protections*, *supra*, at 30–32.

73. Kassin et al., *supra*.

74. *Id.* at 200.

75. *Id.* at 199.

76. See generally White, "*Miranda*'s Failure," *supra*, at 1217–21.

77. In another experimental study, Kassin and Sukel found that "[t]he mere presence of a confession was . . . sufficient to turn acquittal into conviction, irrespective of the contexts in which it was elicited and presented." Saul M. Kassin and Holly Sukel, "Coerced Confessions and the Jury: An Experimental Test of the 'Harmless Error' Rule," 21 *L. and Human Behav.* 27, 42 (1997). Jurors who were exposed to a defendant's confession "did not sufficiently discount" the confession in reaching their verdicts, "even when they saw the confession as coerced, even when the judge ruled the confession inadmissible, and even when participants said that it did not influence their decision-making." *Id.* See also Saul M. Kassin and Lawrence S. Wrightsman, "Prior Confessions and Mock Juror Verdicts," 10 *J. Applied Psychol.* 133 (1980).

78. See James D. Johnson et al., "Justice Is Still Not Colorblind: Differential Racial Effects of Exposure to Inadmissible Evidence," 21 *Personality and Soc. Psychol. Bull.* 893 (1995).

79. See Hart, *supra*.

80. Kassin et al., *supra*, at 187.

Notes to Chapter 4

1. See generally Mark Purdy, "Buddies Show Us the Real Tillman," *San Jose Mercury News*, May 4, 2004; Scott Bordow, "Thousands Pay Tribute to Tillman," *The (Mesa, Arizona) Tribune*, May 4, 2004; Josh White, "Tillman Killed by 'Friendly Fire,'" *Washington Post*, May 30, 2004; Steve Coll, "Army Spun Tale around Ill-Fated Mission," *Washington Post*, Dec. 6, 2004, at A01.

2. Michelle L. Buck and Dale T. Miller, "Reactions to Incongruous Negative Life Events," 7 *Social Justice Research* 29 (1994).

3. Richard Delgado, "Rodrigo's Eleventh Chronicle: Empathy and False Empathy," 84 *Cal. L. Rev.* 61, 76 (1996).

4. *Id.* at 77.

5. Daniel Kahneman and Dale T. Miller, "Norm Theory: Comparing Reality to Its Alternatives," 93 *Psychol. Rev.* 136 (1986).

6. Robert A. Prentice and Jonathan J. Koehler, "A Normality Bias in Legal Decision Making," 88 *Cornell L. Rev.* 583, 639 (2003).

7. Kahneman and Miller, *supra*, at 146.

8. Neal J. Roese, "Counterfactual Thinking," 121 *Psychol. Bull.* 133 (1997).

9. E.g., Prentice and Koehler, *supra*, at 616–17; Barbara A. Spellman and Alexandra Kincannon, "The Relation between Counterfactual ('But For')

and Causal Reasoning: Experimental Findings and Implications for Jurors' Decisions," 64 *L. and Contemporary Problems* 241 (2001).

10. See generally Robert Cowley, ed., *What Ifs? of American History* (2003), and specifically Lawrence Malkin and John F. Stacks, "What If Watergate Were Still Just an Upscale Address?" in that volume. See also Philip E. Tetlock, "Close-Call Counterfactuals and Belief-System Defense: I Was Not Almost Wrong but I Was Almost Right," 75 *J. Personality and Soc. Psychol.* 639 (1998).

11. See Joel T. Johnson, "The Knowledge of What Might Have Been: Affective and Attributional Consequences of Near Outcomes," 12 *Personality and Social Psychology Bulletin* 51 (1986).

12. M. H. Medvec, S. F. Madey, and T. Glovich, "When Less Is More: Counterfactual Thinking and Satisfaction among Olympic Athletes," 69 *J. Personality and Soc. Psychol.* 603–10 (1995).

13. Kahneman and Miller, *supra*, at 142–45.

14. See, e.g., Julia Malone, "Faulty Exit Polls Still Puzzle Experts; Weeks after Election Day, Consortium Trying to Determine Why Numbers Predicted Kerry Win," *Austin American-Statesman*, Nov. 25, 2004; Maeve Reston, "Defeat More Painful after Victory Had Seemed Sure," *Pittsburgh Post-Gazette*, Nov. 4, 2004.

15. Neal Feigenson, *Legal Blame: How Jurors Think and Talk about Accidents* 54 (2000).

16. E.g., *id.* at 53–56.

17. See, e.g., C. Neil Macrae, "A Tale of Two Curries: Counterfactual Thinking and Accident-Related Judgments," 18 *Personality and Soc. Psychol. Bull.* 84 (1992); C. Neil Macrae and Alan B. Milne, "A Curry for Your Thoughts: Empathic Effects on Counterfactual Thinking," 18 *Personality and Soc. Psychol. Bull.* 625 (1992).

18. Kahneman and Miller, *supra*, at 136–37, 146–50.

19. See generally Dale T. Miller and William Turnbull, "The Counterfactual Fallacy: Confusing What Might Have Been with What Ought to Have Been," 4 *Social Justice Research* 1 (1990).

20. As Kahneman and Miller have explained, "An abnormal event is one that has highly available alternatives, whether retrieved or constructed; a normal event mainly evokes representations that resemble it." Kahneman and Miller, *supra*, at 137.

21. See Prentice and Koehler, *supra*, at 640–41.

22. C. Neil Macrae et al., "Counterfactual Thinking and the Perception of Criminal Behaviour," 84 *Brit. J. Psychol.* 221 (1993).

23. See generally Lu-in Wang, "The Complexities of 'Hate,'" 60 *Ohio State L.J.* 799, 821–24 (1999).

24. See Matthew T. Crawford and Dean M. McCrea, "When Mutations Meet Motivations: Attitude Biases in Counterfactual Thought," 40 *J. Experimental Social Psychology* 65 (2004).

25. Christopher T. Burris and Nyla R. Branscombe, "Racism, Counterfactual Thinking, and Judgment Severity," 23 *J. Applied Soc. Psychol.* 980 (1993).

26. Miller and Turnbull, *supra*, at 2 (emphasis in original).

27. Linda Hamilton Krieger, "Civil Rights Perestroika: Intergroup Relations after Affirmative Action," 86 *Cal. L. Rev.* 1253, 1327 (1998).

28. Dale T. Miller and Cathy McFarland, "Counterfactual Thinking and Victim Compensation: A Test of Norm Theory," 12 *Personality and Soc. Psychol. Bull.* 513 (1987).

29. John E. Hilsenrath, "Hard Times Hit Ordinary Joes—Now Unemployment Is Rising for Blue Collar Workers; No Job and No Safety Net?" *Wall Street Journal*, Sept. 10, 2001 (quoting economist Lawrence Katz).

30. Ira Breskin, "A Tale of Joblessness, Long Island Style; Economic Woes Hit Many Corporate Fast-Trackers. Comparable Jobs Are Hard to Find." *Christian Science Monitor*, Aug. 23, 2003 (quoting economist Pearl Kramer). See also, e.g., Steven Greenhouse, "Deciding Who Hurts Most in a Slump," *N.Y. Times*, May 18, 2003; Mark Levitan, Community Service Society, *A Portrait of Inequality: Unemployment and Joblessness in New York City, 2002* (Feb. 2003).

31. What actually happened that night is in dispute, and we may never know the truth. Five young men were convicted in the case and served from seven to thirteen years in prison before their convictions were vacated in December 2002. The Manhattan district attorney joined with defense lawyers in seeking to have the convictions thrown out based on new evidence indicating that a lone attacker—a convicted murderer and rapist—had committed the crime and casting doubt on the reliability of the five defendants' confessions and other evidence that had been presented at trial. See Susan Saulny, "Convictions and Charges Voided in '89 Central Park Jogger Attack," *N.Y. Times*, Dec. 20, 2002; Jim Dwyer, "One Trail, Two Conclusions; Police and Prosecutors May Never Agree on Who Began Jogger Attack," *N.Y. Times*, Feb. 2, 2003.

32. Kimberle Crenshaw, "Mapping the Margins: Intersectionality, Identity Politics, and Violence against Women of Color," 43 *Stan. L. Rev.* 1241, 1267 (1991).

33. *Id.* at 1268.

34. Charlie McCollum, "Discrepancy in Coverage for Two Missing Girls: One White, One Black," *San Jose Mercury News*, July 2, 2002.

35. See Mark Johnson and Annysa Johnson, "2 Missing Girls' Cases

Show Media Disparity: Alexis Gets Little Notice, Utah Girl Widely Covered," *Milwaukee Journal Sentinel*, June 14, 2002.

36. *Id.*

37. McCollum, *supra.*

38. Delgado, *supra*, at 77.

39. Miller and Turnbull, *supra*, at 9.

40. Iris Marion Young, *Justice and the Politics of Difference* 61 (1990). See also Thomas Ashby Wills, "Downward Comparison Principles in Social Psychology," 90 *Psychological Bulletin* 245, 246, 257 (1981).

41. Dorothy E. Roberts, "Foreword: Race, Vagueness, and the Social Meaning of Order-Maintenance Policing," 89 *J. Crim. L. and Criminology* 775, 811–13 (1999).

42. Deseriee A. Kennedy, "Consumer Discrimination: The Limitations of Federal Civil Rights Protection," 66 *Mo. L. Rev.* 275, 303 (2001), quoting Philomena Essed, *Understanding Everyday Racism* 50 (1991).

43. See René Bowser, "Racial Profiling in Health Care: An Institutional Analysis of Medical Treatment Disparities," 7 *Mich. J. Race and L.* 79 (2001).

44. Miller and Turnbull, *supra*, at 9.

45. *Id.*

46. See Nyla R. Branscombe and Julie A. Weir, "Resistance as Stereotype-Inconsistency: Consequences for Judgments of Rape Victims," 11 *J. Soc. and Clinical Psychol.* 80 (1992), quoting Lawrence S. Wrightsman, *Psychology and the Legal System* (1987).

47. See generally, e.g., Linda S. Perloff, "Social Comparison and Illusions of Invulnerability to Negative Life Events," in *Coping with Negative Life Events: Clinical and Social Psychological Perspectives* 218 (C. R. Snyder and Carol E. Ford, eds., 1987); Thomas Ashby Wills, "Downward Comparison as a Coping Mechanism," in *Coping with Negative Life Events*, at 243–46.

48. See generally Lu-in Wang, "The Transforming Power of 'Hate': Social Cognition Theory and the Harms of Bias-Related Crime," 71 *S. Cal. L. Rev.* 47, 94–97, 126–27 (1997).

49. Roese, *supra.*

50. Gary L. Wells and Igor Gavanski, "Mental Simulation of Causality," 56 *J. Personality and Soc. Psychol.* 161 (1989).

51. Prentice and Koehler, *supra*, at 617.

52. Wells and Gavanski, *supra.*

53. See Macrae et al., *supra.*

54. Miller and Turnbull, *supra*, at 13.

55. *Id.* at 14.

56. See, for example, Rachel McCloy and Ruth M. J. Byrne, "Counterfactual Thinking about Controllable Events," 28 *Memory and Cognition* 1071 (2000).

57. Prentice and Koehler, *supra*.

58. *Id.* at 628.

59. *Id.* at 631.

60. *Id.* at 595.

61. *Id.*

62. *Id.* at 632–33.

63. See, e.g., James B. Jacobs and Kimberly Potter, *Hate Crimes: Criminal Law and Identity Politics* 81 (1998).

64. See Anthony C. Thompson, "Stopping the Usual Suspects: Race and the Fourth Amendment," 74 *N.Y.U. L. Rev.* 956, 972 (1999).

65. See, e.g., Deborah Brake, "The Cruelest of the Gender Police: Student-to-Student Sexual Harassment and Anti-Gay Peer Harassment under Title IX," I *Georgetown J. Gender and L.* 37, 55–59 (1999); Deborah Brake, "The Struggle for Sex Equality in Sport and the Theory behind Title IX," 34 *U. Mich. J. L. Reform* 13, 92–107 (2001); Wang, "The Complexities of 'Hate,'" *supra*, at 876.

66. See, e.g., Krieger, "Civil Rights Perestroika," *supra*, at 1311.

67. David A. Harris, *Profiles in Injustice: Why Racial Profiling Cannot Work* 15 (2003).

68. *Id.* at 39–41. See also Thompson, *supra*, at 989.

69. Harris, *Profiles in Injustice*, *supra*, at 27. See also David Cole, *No Equal Justice: Race and Class in the American Criminal Justice System* 53 (1999).

70. Harris, *supra*, at 15.

71. *Id.* at 79.

72. *Id.* at 78–79.

73. See *id.* at 75–78.

74. See, e.g., Ushma Patel, "Thumbs Up, Down in Area; Residents Divided over Ashcroft Plan," *Atlanta Journal-Constitution*, June 6, 2002; Priya Rai, "I Once Believed in Diversity; but Then Came September 11," *Hartford Courant*, June 9, 2002.

75. Lu-in Wang, "'Suitable Targets'? Parallels and Connections between 'Hate' Crimes and 'Driving while Black,'" 6 *Mich. J. Race and L.* 209, 232 (2001) (citations omitted).

76. David A. Harris, "The Stories, the Statistics, and the Law: Why 'Driving while Black' Matters," 84 *Minn. L. Rev.* 265, 298–99 (1999).

77. *Id.* at 274. See also Katheryn K. Russell, *The Color of Crime: Racial Hoaxes, White Fear, Black Protectionism, Police Harassment, and Other Macroaggressions* 34 (1998).

78. Harris, *Profiles in Injustice*, *supra*, at 102.

79. See generally *id.* at 102–06.

80. See Darren K. Carlson, "Racial Profiling Seen as Pervasive, Unjust," Gallup Poll, July 20, 2004; Jack Ludwig, "Americans See Racial Profiling as Widespread," Gallup Poll, May 13, 2003.

81. Darren K. Carlson, "Racial Divide: Crime and Police Protection," Gallup Poll, Oct. 29, 2002; Harris, *Profiles in Injustice*, *supra*, at 121–24.

82. See generally *id.* at 117–28.

83. Bowser, *supra*, at 98.

84. See Gary David Comstock, *Violence against Lesbians and Gay Men* 92–93 (1990); Wang, "The Complexities of 'Hate,'" *supra*, at 877; Eric Weissman, "Kids Who Attack Gays," *Christopher Street*, Aug. 1978, at 9, reprinted in *Hate Crimes: Confronting Violence against Lesbians and Gay Men* 170 (Gregory M. Herek and Kevin T. Berrill, eds., 1992).

85. See, e.g., Cynthia Grant Bowman, "Street Harassment and the Informal Ghettoization of Women," 106 *Harv. L. Rev.* 517, 541–43 (1993).

86. See Prentice and Koehler, *supra*, at 635–37.

87. See, e.g., Meritor Savings Bank v. Vinson, 477 U.S. 57 (1986); Susan Estrich, "Rape," 95 *Yale L. J.* 1087, 1094, 1121–32 (1986).

88. Nyla R. Branscombe et al., "Rape and Accident Counterfactuals: Who Might Have Done Otherwise and Would It Have Changed the Outcome?" 26 *J. Applied Social Psychology* 1042, 1063 (1996).

89. Roberts, *supra*, at 807.

90. Harris, "Why 'Driving while Black' Matters," *supra*, at 268.

91. Wang, "The Complexities of 'Hate,'" *supra*, at 877 (citations omitted).

92. See generally Lynette Sharp Penya, "Counterfactuals and Juror Decision-Making: How the Alternatives Jurors Entertain Affect Their Judgments in Sexual Harassment Cases," *National Institute on Sexual Harassment: A Multi-Disciplinary View of the New Generation of Sexual Harassment Policies and Procedures and a Trial of a Sexual Harassment Case* (American Bar Association Center for Continuing Legal Education National Institute, 1998) (available on Westlaw, N98SHCB ABA-LGLED F-9).

93. See generally Jacobs and Potter, *supra*, at 79–91.

94. See Stephen D. Goldinger et al., "'Blaming the Victim' under Memory Load," 14 *Psychol. Sci.* 81 (2003).

95. Ronnie Janoff-Bulman, "The Aftermath of Victimization: Rebuilding Shattered Assumptions," in *Trauma and Its Wake: The Study and Treatment of Post-Traumatic Stress Disorder* 15, 20 (Charles R. Figley, ed., 1985).

96. See generally *id.* at 18–22; Ronnie Janoff-Bulman and Irene Hanson

Frieze, "A Theoretical Perspective for Understanding Reactions to Victimization," 39 *J. Soc. Issues* 1 (1983); Shelley E. Taylor and Jonathan D. Brown, "Illusion and Well-Being: A Social Psychological Perspective on Mental Health," 103 *Psychol. Bull.* 193 (1988).

97. See generally Irene Hanson Frieze, Martin S. Greenberg, and Sharon Hymer, "Describing the Crime Victim: Psychological Reactions to Victimization, 18 *Prof. Psychol.: Res. and Prac.* 299 (1987); Martin Symonds, "The 'Second Injury' to Victims," *Evaluation and Change*, Special Issue 1980, at 36; Wang, "The Transforming Power of 'Hate,'" *supra*, at 105–08.

98. Shelley E. Taylor, Joanne V. Wood, and Rosemary Lichtman, "It Could Be Worse: Selective Evaluation as a Response to Victimization," 39 *J. Social Issues* 19, 23 (1983).

99. See Linda Garnets, Gregory M. Herek, and Barrie Levy, "Violence and Victimization of Lesbians and Gay Men: Mental Health Consequences," 5 *J. Interpersonal Violence* 366, 374 (1990); Gregory M. Herek, "Hate Crimes against Lesbians and Gay Men: Issues for Research and Policy," 44 *Am. Psychologist* 948 (1989).

100. Cf. Bowman, *supra*, at 541.

101. Patricia Williams, "Spirit-Murdering the Messenger: The Discourse of Fingerpointing as the Law's Response to Racism," 42 *U. Miami L. Rev.* 127, 136 (1987).

102. Branscombe and Weir, *supra*, at 84

103. Cf. Miller and Turnbull, *supra*, at 4.

104. Daniel Kahneman and Amos Tversky, "The Simulation Heuristic," in *Judgment under Uncertainty: Heuristics and Bias* 201, 204–05 (Daniel Kahneman, Paul Slovic, and Amos Tversky, eds., 1982). See also Feigenson, *supra*, at 53–54.

105. Branscombe and Weir, *supra*, at 84.

106. *Id.* at 96.

107. *Id.* at 97.

108. Doré Butler and Florence L. Geis, "Nonverbal Affect Responses to Male and Female Leaders: Implications for Leadership Evaluations," 58 *J. Personality and Social Psychology* 48 (1990).

109. See, e.g., john a. powell, "Rights Talk/Free Speech and Equality," 1992/1993 *Ann. Surv. Am. L.* 587, 589–90; Lena Williams, *It's the Little Things: The Everyday Interactions That Get under the Skin of Blacks and Whites* 41–43 (2000).

110. Herek, "Hate Crimes against Lesbians and Gay Men," *supra*, at 948.

111. Pat K. Chew, "Asian Americans: The 'Reticent' Minority and Their Paradoxes," 36 *Wm. and Mary L. Rev.* 1, 69–70 (1994).

Notes to Chapter 5

1. Because most of the empirical studies have focused on Black-White disparities, and because of the unique history of African Americans and medicine in this country, this discussion focuses on differences between the health outcomes and medical treatment of Blacks and Whites. Some of the points made in this chapter, however, undoubtedly apply to other social groups.

2. See, e.g., W. Michael Byrd and Lynda A. Clayton, *An American Health Dilemma: A Medical History of African Americans and the Problem of Race* 29–33 (2000).

3. Institute of Medicine, *Unequal Treatment: Confronting Racial and Ethnic Disparities in Health Care* 138 (2002) (emphasis added).

For fuller discussion and more detailed examination of the empirical evidence of racial disparities in health care, see, e.g., René Bowser, "Racial Profiling in Health Care: An Institutional Analysis of Medical Treatment Disparities," 7 *Mich. J. Race and L.* 79, 83–91 (2001); Mary Crossley, "Infected Judgment: Legal Responses to Physician Bias," 48 *Vill. L. Rev.* 195, 201–17 (2003); Inst. Med., *supra*, at App. B; Barbara A. Noah, "Racial Disparities in the Delivery of Health Care," 35 *San Diego L. Rev.* 135, 138–56 (1998); Michael S. Shin, "Redressing Wounds: Finding a Legal Framework to Remedy Racial Disparities in Medical Care," 90 *Cal. L. Rev.* 2047, 2054–58 (2002); Sidney D. Watson, "Race, Ethnicity and Quality of Care: Inequalities and Incentives," 27 *Am. J. L. and Med.* 203, 205–09 (2001).

4. See, e.g., Roberto Bernabei et al., "Management of Pain in Elderly Patients with Cancer," 279 *JAMA* 1877 (1998); Edward Guadagnoli et al., "The Influence of Race on the Use of Surgical Procedures for Treatment of Peripheral Vascular Disease of the Lower Extremities," 130 *Arch. Surgery* 381 (1995); Kevin A. Schulman et al., "The Effect of Race and Sex on Physicians' Recommendations for Cardiac Catheterization," 340 *New Eng. J. Med.* 618 (1999); Knox H. Todd et al., "Ethnicity and Analgesic Practice," 35 *Annals Emergency Med.* 11 (2000). See also Knox H. Todd et al., "Ethnicity as a Risk Factor for Inadequate Emergency Department Analgesia," 269 *JAMA* 1537 (1993).

5. See generally, e.g., Erica Goode, "Minorities' Care for Mental Ills Is Called Inferior," *N.Y. Times*, Aug. 27, 2001; William B. Lawson et al., "Race as a Factor in Inpatient and Outpatient Admissions and Diagnoses," 45 *Hosp. and Community Psychiatry* 72 (1994); Thomas W. Pavkov et al., "Psychiatric Diagnoses and Racial Bias: An Empirical Investigation," 20 *Prof. Psychol.: Research and Practice* 364 (1989); Steven P. Segal et al., "Race, Quality of Care, and Antipsychotic Prescribing Practices in Psychi-

atric Emergency Services," 47 *Psychiatric Services* 282 (1996); Jay C. Wade, "Institutional Racism: An Analysis of the Mental Health System," 63 *Am. J. Orthopsychiatry* 536 (1993); Arthur L. Whaley, "Racism in the Provision of Mental Health Services: A Social Cognitive Analysis," 68 *Am. J. Orthopsychiatry* 47, 52 (1998).

6. Inst. Med., *supra*, at 140.

7. See, e.g., Council on Ethical and Judicial Affairs of the American Medical Association, "Black-White Disparities in Health Care," 263 *JAMA* 2344, 2346 (1990); Editorial, "Racial Disparities in Medical Care," 344 *New Eng. J. Med.* 1471 (2001).

8. Sally Satel, *PC M.D.: How Political Correctness Is Corrupting Medicine* 4–5 (2000).

9. See, e.g., M. Gregg Bloche, "Race and Discretion in American Medicine," I *Yale J. Health Pol'y, L., and Ethics* 95, 97–99 (2001).

10. See Satel, *supra*, at 166–70. But see Bloche, *supra*, at 105; Bowser, "Racial Profiling in Health Care," *supra*, at 92–95.

11. See, e.g., Inst. Med., *supra*, at 127; Watson, *supra*, at 208–09. For a review of such studies, see Inst. Med., *supra*, at 32–59 and App. B.

12. See Satel, *supra*, at 166.

13. See generally Vernellia R. Randall, "Slavery, Segregation and Racism: Trusting the Health Care System Ain't Always Easy! An African American Perspective on Bioethics," 15 *St. Louis U. Pub. L. Rev.* 191 (1996).

14. Crossley, *supra*, at 222.

15. See Bowser, "Racial Profiling in Health Care," *supra*, at 93–94.

16. See, e.g., Jeff Whittle et al., "Do Patient Preferences Contribute to Racial Differences in Cardiovascular Use?" 12 *J. Gen. Internal Med.* 267, 271 (1997).

17. Jeffrey N. Katz, Commentary, "Patient Preferences and Health Disparities," 286 *JAMA* 1506 (2001).

18. See, e.g., Bloche, *supra*, at 98; Crossley, *supra*, at 218.

19. See, e.g., Inst. Med., *supra*, at 132; Noah, *supra*, at 165.

20. Bowser, "Racial Profiling in Health Care," *supra*, at 97, 115–24.

21. Bloche, *supra*, at 121.

22. See Bowser, "Racial Profiling in Health Care," *supra*, at 119; Steven H. Caldwell and Rebecca Popenoe, "Perceptions and Misperceptions of Skin Color," 122 *Annals Internal Med.* 614 (1995); Thomas Finacune and Joseph A. Carnese, "Racial Bias in Presentation of Cases," 5 *J. Gen. Internal Med.* 120 (1990).

23. Delthia Ricks, "'Silent Curriculum': Racial, Ethnic Bias Hazardous to Health," *Pittsburgh Post-Gazette*, Jan. 5, 1999, at D-3 (quoting Dr. Judith Gwathmey). See also Caldwell and Popenoe, *supra*, at 616.

24. Bowser, "Racial Profiling in Health Care," *supra*, at 98.

25. See *id.* at 110–11, quoting Mindy Thompson Fullilove, "Deconstructing Race in Medical Research," 148 *Archives Pediatrics Adolescent Med.* 1014, 1014–15 (1994); René Bowser, "Racial Bias in Medical Treatment," 105 *Dick. L. Rev.* 365, 374–75 (2001).

26. Stephen B. Thomas, "The Color Line: Race Matters in the Elimination of Health Disparities," 91 *Am. J. Pub. Health* 1046, 1047 (2001). For a thorough examination of race in medicine, including normative recommendations on the circumstances under which it is, and is not, appropriately utilized, see Erik Lillquist and Charles A. Sullivan, "The Law and Genetics of Racial Profiling in Medicine," 39 *Harv. C.R.-C.L. L. Rev.* 391 (2004).

27. See, e.g, Bowser, "Racial Profiling in Health Care," *supra*, at 104–05. See also Byrd and Clayton, *supra*, at 106–08, 207–08, and 258–59; John Hoberman, *Darwin's Athletes: How Sport Has Damaged Black America and Preserved the Myth of Race* 171–72 (1997); David Barton Smith, *Health Care Divided: Race and Healing a Nation* 21–22 (1999).

28. *Id.* at 24.

29. See *id.* at 25–26.

30. See generally Vicki S. Freimuth et al., "African Americans' Views on Research and the Tuskegee Syphilis Study," 52 *Soc. Sci. Med.* 797 (2001).

31. Laura M. Bogart and Sheryl Thorburn, "Are HIV/AIDS Conspiracy Beliefs a Barrier to HIV Prevention among African Americans?" 38 *J. Acquired Immune Deficiency Syndromes* 213 (2005).

32. See, e.g., Smith, *supra*, at 9–33; Watson, *supra*, at 210–13.

33. See Bowser, "Racial Profiling in Health Care," *supra*, at 102–15.

34. See, e.g., Bloche, *supra*, at 104–05; Bowser, "Racial Profiling in Health Care," *supra*, at 109.

35. See, e.g., *id.* at 108–10; Crossley, *supra*, at 204–05.

36. See Michelle van Ryn and Jane Burke, "The Effect of Patient Race and Socioeconomic Status on Physicians' Perceptions of Patients," 50 *Soc. Sci. Med.* 813, 814 (2000).

37. See John M. Eisenberg, "Sociologic Influences on Decision-Making by Clinicians," 90 *Annals Internal Med.* 957 (1979); Barbara Gerbert, "Perceived Likeability and Competence of Simulated Patients: Influence on Physicians' Management Plans," 18 *Soc. Sci. Med.* 1053, 1053–54 (1984); Elizabeth M. Hooper et al., "Patient Characteristics That Influence Physician Behavior," 20 *Med. Care* 630 (1982). See also Crossley, *supra*, at 231–36; Saif S. Rathone et al., "The Effects of Patient Sex and Race on Medical Students' Ratings of Quality of Life," 108 *Am. J. Med.* 561 (2000).

38. See generally van Ryn and Burke, *supra*.

39. *Id.* at 815.

40. See Shin, *supra*, at 2065.

41. Bloche, *supra*, at 104.

42. See van Ryn and Burke, *supra*, at 824. Cf. Whaley, *supra*, at 48.

43. van Ryn and Burke, *supra*.

44. Eisenberg, *supra*, at 958.

45. See Judith A. Hall et al., "Physicians' Liking for Their Patients: More Evidence for the Role of Affect in Medical Care," 12 *Health Psychology* 140, 143 (1993).

46. Linda S. Fidell, "Sex Role Stereotypes and the American Physician," 4 *Psych. Women Q.* 313, 322 (1980). See also Crossley, *supra*, at 230.

47. See Shin, *supra*, at 2074–75.

48. Bloche, *supra*, at 97.

49. Ana I. Balsa et al., "Clinical Uncertainty and Healthcare Disparities," 29 *Am. J. L. and Med.* 203, 207 (2003).

50. See Daniel T. Gilbert and J. Gregory Hixon, "The Trouble of Thinking: Activation and Application of Stereotypic Beliefs," 60 *J. Personality and Soc. Psychol.* 509 (1991).

51. See, e.g., Balsa et al., *supra*, at 402; Bloche, *supra*, at 104–05; Shin, *supra*, at 2074.

52. Inst. Med., *supra*, at 132.

53. Eisenberg, *supra*, at 957.

54. See, e.g., Jozien Bensing, "Doctor-Patient Communication and the Quality of Care," 32 *Soc. Sci. Med.* 1301, 1305–06 (1991); Sherrie Kaplan et al., "Patient and Visit Characteristics Related to Physicians' Participatory Decision-Making Style: Results from the Medical Outcomes Study," 33 *Med. Care* 1176, 1177 (1995); Joan J. Mathews, "The Communication Process in Clinical Settings," 17 *Soc. Sci. Med.* 1371 (1983); Howard Waitzkin, "Information Giving in Medical Care," 26 *J. Health and Soc. Behavior* 81 (1985).

55. See, e.g., Eisenberg, *supra*, at 962; Gerbert, *supra*, at 1057; van Ryn and Burke, *supra*, at 823.

56. See, e.g., Waitzkin, *supra*, at 93; cf. van Ryn and Burke, *supra*, at 823.

57. See Bensing, *supra*, at 1307–08.

58. See C. Knight Aldrich, *The Medical Interview: Gateway to the Doctor-Patient Interview* 21–22 (2d ed. 1999); Bensing, *supra*, at 1305.

59. See *id.* at 1308.

60. See Hall et al., *supra*, at 144.

61. See *id.*; Matthews, *supra*; van Ryn and Burke, *supra*.

62. See generally, e.g., Association of American Medical Colleges, *Mi-*

nority Students in Medical Education: Facts and Figures XII (2002); Stanley S. Bergen Jr., "Underrepresented Minorities in Medicine," 284 *JAMA* 1138 (2000); David M. Carlisle and Jill E. Gardner, "The Entry of African American Students into U.S. Medical Schools: An Evaluation of Recent Trends," 90 *J. Nat'l Med. Ass'n* 466 (1998); The Sullivan Commission on Diversity in the Healthcare Workforce, *Missing Persons: Minorities in the Health Professions* (2004).

63. Inst. Med., *supra*, at 146 (citing Lisa Cooper-Patrick et al., "Race, Gender, and Partnership in the Patient-Physician Relationship," 282 *JAMA* 583 (1999)).

64. See, e.g., Cooper-Patrick et al., *supra*; Hall et al., *supra*, at 140; Kaplan et al., *supra*, at 1179–80; van Ryn and Burke, *supra*, at 823; Waitzkin, *supra*, at 93.

65. See, e.g., Barbara A. Noah, Book Review, "The Invisible Patient," 2002 *U. Ill. L. Rev.* 121, 143–44; cf. Shin, *supra*, at 2074–75.

66. Neil S. Calman, "Out of the Shadow: A White Inner-City Doctor Wrestles with Racial Prejudice," 9 *Health Affairs* 170 (2000).

67. Balsa et al., *supra*, at 210.

68. Shin, *supra*, at 128.

69. Inst. Med., *supra*, at 128.

70. Theodore R. Brooks, "Pitfalls in Communication with Hispanic and African-American Patients: Do Translators Help or Harm?" 84 *J. Nat'l Med. Ass'n* 941 (1992); Jeffrey A. Ferguson et al., "Racial Disparity in Cardiac Decisionmaking: Results from Patient Focus Groups," 158 *Arch. Intern. Med.* 1450 (1998).

71. See John Hoberman, "Culture Watch: A Medical Prescription for More Racial Sensitivity," *Newsday*, Jan. 10, 1999, at B06; see also Ferguson et al., *supra*, at 1451.

72. See Whaley, *supra*, at 51. Cf. Mark Snyder, "Motivational Foundations of Behavioral Confirmation," 25 *Advances in Experimental Soc. Psychol.* 67, 93–94 (1992).

73. Waitzkin, *supra*, at 82.

74. Cathy J. Jones, "Autonomy and Informed Consent in Medical Decisionmaking: Toward a New Self-Fulfilling Prophecy," 47 *Wash. and Lee L. Rev.* 379, 407 (1990).

75. Mathews, *supra*, at 1376, quoting E. Friedson, *Professional Dominance* 142 (1970).

76. See Eisenberg, *supra*, at 957.

77. Cf. Erving Goffman, *Stigma: Notes on the Management of Spoiled Identity* 7–9 (1963).

78. Fidell, *supra*, at 318–19.

79. Mathews, *supra*, at 1372, quoting Erving Goffman, *Asylums* 84 (1961).

80. Mathews, *supra*, at 1372.

81. *Id.* at 1375.

82. *Id.* See also Jones, *supra*, at 425.

83. Snyder, *supra*, at 93–94.

84. Whaley, *supra*.

85. Arthur L. Whaley, "The Culturally-Sensitive Diagnostic Interview Research Project: A Study on the Psychiatric Misdiagnosis of African American Patients," 8 *African American Research Perspectives* 57 (2002).

86. David Sue and Stanley Sue, "Cultural Factors in the Clinical Assessment of Asian Americans," 55 *J. Consulting and Clinical Psychol.* 479 (1987).

87. Bloche, *supra*, at 103; Jones, *supra*, at 387; Mathews, *supra*, at 1372; Noah, *supra*, at 477.

88. Bloche, *supra*, at 105; Shin, *supra*, at 2075.

89. Balsa et al., *supra*, at 212; Ana I. Balsa and Thomas G. McGuire, "Prejudice, Clinical Uncertainty and Stereotyping as Sources of Health Disparities," 22 *J. Health Economics* 89, 103–06 (2003).

90. Bowser, "Racial Bias in Medical Treatment," *supra*, at 370.

91. Linda Hamilton Krieger, "Civil Rights Perestroika: Intergroup Relations after Affirmative Action," 86 *Cal. L. Rev.* 1251, 1313 (1998) (emphasis in original).

92. 42 U.S.C. § 2000d (2001).

93. See Alexander v. Sandoval, 532 U.S. 275 (2001). See also Crossley, *supra*, at 280–91; Noah, *supra*, at 163–65; Shin, *supra*, at 2076–79.

Moreover, even these exceedingly narrow avenues for redress might not be available to some plaintiffs who seek to sue individual practitioners, for Title VI's requirement that the defendant receive federal financial assistance has been interpreted to exclude Medicare payments from that category, "put[ting] private physicians out of Title VI's reach," Bloche, *supra*, at 111, and an equal protection claim would require the plaintiff to establish "state action"—a difficult element to prove in a claim that focuses on a practitioner's clinical decisions, see Noah, *supra*, at 164.

94. Crossley, *supra*, at 281.

95. Noah, *supra*, at 164.

96. See, e.g., Crossley, *supra*, at 280–96. In addition, and again because medical decision making is complex and inherently uncertain and medical decision makers are accorded a great deal of discretion, diagnosis and treatment decisions that have been influenced by racial bias (and therefore that might have come out differently were the patient of a different race) are not

likely to be unacceptable under noncivil rights causes of action that might otherwise apply. In a medical malpractice case, for example, the patient must establish both causation and the defendant's failure to conform to the applicable standard of care. It is extremely difficult to establish causation because the requisite data comparing the efficacy of alternative treatments often does not exist. Furthermore, even if a decision has been influenced by the patient's race and is not ideal for that individual, it is unlikely to fall outside the acceptable limits of clinical discretion. See, e.g., Bloche, *supra*, at 109; Crossley, *supra*, at 244–48 and 261–63; Shin, *supra*, at 2079–80.

Notes to Chapter 6

1. Robert K. Merton, "The Self-Fulfilling Prophecy," 8 *Antioch Review* 193, 197 (1948).
2. Jody David Armour, *Negrophobia and Reasonable Racism: The Hidden Costs of Being Black in America* 139 (1997).
3. *Id.* at 149.
4. *Id.* at 151–53.
5. Peter D. Blanck, Robert Rosenthal, and L. H. Cordell, Note, "The Appearance of Justice: Judges' Verbal and Nonverbal Behavior in Criminal Jury Trials," 89 *Stan. L. Rev.* 89 (1985); Allen J. Hart, "Naturally Occurring Expectation Effects," 68 *J. Personality and Soc. Psychol.* 109 (1995).
6. Andrea M. Halverson et al., "Reducing the Biasing Effects of Judges' Nonverbal Behavior with Simplified Jury Instructions," 82 *J. Applied Psychology* 590 (1997).
7. See generally Nyla R. Branscombe et al., "Rape and Accident Counterfactuals: Who Might Have Done Otherwise and Would It Have Changed the Outcome?" 26 *J. Applied Psychology* 1042, 1061–64 (1996).
8. See Lynette Sharp Penya, "Counterfactuals and Juror Decision-Making: How the Alternatives Jurors Entertain Affect Their Judgments in Sexual Harassment Cases," *National Institute on Sexual Harassment: A Multi-Disciplinary View of the New Generation of Sexual Harassment Policies and Procedures and a Trial of a Sexual Harassment Case* (American Bar Association Center for Continuing Legal Education National Institute 1998) (available on Westlaw, N98SHCB ABA-LGLED F-9).
9. See Branscombe et al., *supra*, at 1062–63.
10. See, e.g., M. Gregg Bloche, "Race and Discretion in American Medicine," I *Yale J. Health Pol'y, L., and Ethics* 95, 117 (2001); René Bowser, "Racial Profiling in Health Care: An Institutional Analysis of Medical Treatment Disparities," 7 *Mich. J. Race and L.* 79, 125–32 (2001); Mary Crossley, "Infected Judgment: Legal Responses to Physician Bias," 48 *Vill.*

L. Rev. 195, 296–302 (2003); Barbara A. Noah, "Racial Disparities in the Delivery of Health Care," 35 *San Diego L. Rev.* 135, 169–70 (1998); Sidney D. Watson, "Race, Ethnicity and Quality of Care: Inequalities and Incentives," 27 *Am. J. L. and Med.* 203, 204–05 (2001). But see Michael S. Shin, Note, "Redressing Wounds: Finding a Legal Framework to Remedy Racial Disparities in Medical Care," 90 *Cal. L. Rev.* 2047, 2096–100 (2002).

11. Watson, *supra*, at 211.

12. Simkins v. Moses H. Cone Memorial Hospital, 323 F.2d 959 (4th Cir. 1963).

13. Watson, *supra*, at 212–13 (citing David Barton Smith, *Health Care Divided: Race and Healing a Nation* 82 (1999)).

14. Watson, *supra*, at 212–15. See also Smith, *supra*, at 141.

15. Watson, *supra*, at 215–16.

16. *Id.*

17. Bloche, *supra*, at 121 (emphasis added).

18. See Bowser, *supra*, at 126–28; Crossley, *supra*, at 298–99; Noah, *supra*, at 174–75; Watson, *supra*, at 223–24.

19. Bowser, *supra*, at 128–29.

20. Watson, *supra*, at 223.

21. Bloche, *supra*, at 117. See also Crossley, *supra*, at 301.

22. *Id.*

23. Bloche, *supra*, at 117.

24. Crossley, *supra*, at 300–01.

25. Bloche, *supra*, at 118.

26. *Id.* at 118–19.

27. Watson, *supra*, at 204, 224.

28. René Bowser, "Racial Bias in Medical Treatment," 105 *Dick. L. Rev.* 365, 370 (2001).

29. Merton, *supra*, at 209.

30. David A. Harris, *Profiles in Injustice: Why Racial Profiling Cannot Work* 146 (2002).

31. See *id.* at 169–92.

32. *Id.* at 155–61.

33. *Id.* at 162.

34. *Id.* at 165–69.

35. Merton, *supra*, at 197.

Index

About the Author

Lu-in Wang is Professor of Law at the University of Pittsburgh School of Law, and the author of *Hate Crimes Law* (1994).